THE TEACHER IS THE KEY

THE TEACHER IS THE KEY

A Practical Guide for Teaching the Adolescent with Learning Difficulties

Ken Weber
University of Toronto

LOVE PUBLISHING COMPANY
Denver, Colorado 80222

Published in the United States of America by Love Publishing Company, Denver, Colorado 80222.

First printing, January, 1983.

ISBN 0-89108-117-8

Canadian Cataloguing in Publication Data

Weber, K. J. (Kenneth Jerome), 1940–
The teacher is the key

(The Teacher is the key)
ISBN 0-458-95310-5

1. Slow learning children. 2. Problem children - Education. I. Title. II. Series.

LC4661.W42 371.92′63 C82-094271-5

Cover design: John Ford

For Cecile

The events described in this book are true.
The names have been changed because kids
really are innocent most of the time.

K.J.W.

CONTENTS

THE TEACHER IS THE KEY

PART A

THE TEACHER AND THE ADOLESCENT WITH LEARNING DIFFICULTIES

CHAPTER 1

WHY THE TEACHER IS THE KEY

VIRGINIA WAS six years old when her parents were told she had cancer. Leukemia, the doctors said. Not one of the virulent types; in fact, it was the mildest form the disease could take. Virginia was taken out of school for three months for intensive medical treatment. On her programme of chemotherapy, she lost weight, she lost energy, and, most devastating of all to Virginia, she lost her hair.

By the time the doctors declared the disease to be in remission and Virginia was deemed ready to return to school, certain facts were obvious to everyone. One was that Virginia's cheery disposition made her able to handle the fact of cancer; another was that her curious and quick mind enabled her to handle the time lost in school. What she could not face was the crushing embarrassment of returning to school bald.

Enter Virginia's teacher. When she learned of the problem, she approached her grade one class with the enthusiastic announcement that next Monday—the date of Virginia's proposed return to school—they were going to start learning all about hats. Everyone was to wear a favourite hat to class and, not only this, the hat could be worn indefinitely.

On the following Monday, Virginia returned—hesitant, tentative, and wearing a hat. But her hat was only one of many. Instead of being isolated by her appearance, she was instantly and smoothly one of the group again. Within a week the transition was complete and Virginia was forgetting to wear her hat as frequently as her classmates.

Virginia's teacher did not win an award for her simple but brilliant tactic. She didn't expect or even want one. In fact, what she did is something that most teachers would regard as fairly normal in the course of events: a student had a difficulty and needed special accommodation, so the teacher acted to provide that special accommodation in the best interests of all concerned. There is no mention of this kind of strategy in a curriculum outline, nor is it detailed in any list of teacher technologies.

It's just something that teachers do. Perceiving, analyzing, and responding to a need that seems to have nothing to do with a student's intellectual growth is part of a teacher's daily role. It's why teachers can never be replaced by machines. It's why the teacher is the key.

Because of Virginia's illness and tender age, her teacher's action may seem to merit applause, but no more so than the teacher's action in the following situation.

The Teacher as Facilitator

The school Molly attended is specifically designed for adult basic education. Some of the students have never been to school at all. Some have had several years of secondary schooling, yet need to learn to read and write. Others are quite literate. All the students have some kind of educational difficulty.

Molly, in many ways, was typical. She was in her late thirties, could vaguely remember dropping out of school around grade four or five, and had reached a point in her life where, if she was to have any control of her life, she needed more education. Most of her classmates were unemployed. In this sense, Molly was atypical. She was working—as a prostitute.

The immediate goal for Molly was to develop her math and language skills so that she could enter a hairdresser training programme. Twice she had tried the entrance examination and twice had failed badly, even though her teacher was convinced that she was more than ready. With her confidence gone and hopes fading, Molly was at her lowest ebb when her teacher intervened.

Suspecting a severe case of test anxiety, the teacher obtained a copy of the test and, with the consent of the hairdresser training group, recopied the test, inserting portions of it randomly in Molly's daily schoolwork. Unaware that she was doing test items, Molly came through with an almost perfect score, and her admission to the hairdressing programme was assured.

No matter what a student's age, no matter what the level of motivation and desire, if an educational "problem" is part of that student's makeup, then the gap between the reality of the present and the dream of the future is huge indeed. For such a student, a teacher is the only link; in many ways, the only hope. There is no one else who understands. For students with learning problems, teachers are much more than instructors. They are mediators, counsellors, motivators, and, perhaps most of all, facilitators. What Molly's teacher did here was to facilitate the demands of a process so that Molly's natural ability would not be submerged by her fear.

There was nothing exceptional about this. Teachers do it all the time, especially for students with learning problems. For these students, every learning challenge is a kaleidoscope, an awesome display of demands with facets shooting off in every direction. Only a teacher can reorganize and rearrange that kaleidoscope into a pattern that makes sense, into a sequence with a beginning, middle, and end, into a structure that reduces the scope of the challenge to manageable units. No curriculum and no administrative scheme can accomplish this. Only a teacher can.

The Teacher as Controller of Time

Learning problems generate another unique role for the teacher—that of controlling time. Very often, an adolescent demonstrates educational difficulties because of an inability to adjust to the rhythm and pace of school. A classic example is Burgess, one of my all-time favourite students.

By the age of 15, Burgess had served notice on the world that it had no force strong enough to move him at anything but his own, predetermined speed. He was, without a doubt, the slowest—physically slowest—human being I have ever met. For Burgess, urgency did not exist and acceleration was unattainable. His classmates swore that turning his head to sneeze gave him jet lag! And of course, he was immune to clocks and calendars. He never once, in the year I taught him, completed a piece of work within the assigned period. Nor did he ever arrive for class in time. He would ease into the room, well after class had begun, stick his hands in his pockets, and do a slow but complete 360-degree examination of his environment. Then, assured he'd made the right choice, he would slant toward his seat. One morning in February, on a day when I should have stayed home to nurse a bad cold, Burgess showed up a full hour late. No late slip. No admission slip. No apology. He just stood there. It was too much. "YOU SHOULD HAVE BEEN HERE AT NINE O'CLOCK!" I barked.

"Why?" he said, "what happened?"

So much for the anxiety I was able to stimulate in Burgess! But there was more to him than lack of speed. He was also engaging, pleasant, honest, and, according to one of his technical teachers, moderately gifted in certain manual skills. Burgess, today, is a watchmaker. The irony is inescapable.

In school, however, Burgess was a problem. He had a learning difficulty—or so the file on him indicated. According to the standardized tests which measured such things as reading, he was several grade levels below expectation for his age. His I.Q. results implied mental retardation. Yet, there was a curious discrepancy between these figures and his school achievement. Despite his reported reading level of Grade 3.2 (approximately that of a nine year old), Burgess had B grades in both literature and science. In one technical course he had an A grade, but in mathematics and physical education he was below standard.

It was a matter of time and pace. Physical education for Burgess was almost a foreign language, so "below standard" was understandable there. And because his mathematics programme was built on timed units and standardized, timed tests, Burgess couldn't cope. His literature and science courses, on the other hand, were evaluated by means of open-ended projects with flexible submission dates. With these subjects, his success was evident. Burgess was that kind of student for whom the teacher becomes a shaper of time.

Not all students of this type are at the lethargic extreme of the scale like Burgess. Some are at the opposite end and require yet another set of strategies. However, what both extremes have in common is an inability, or an unwillingness, to yield to the demands of pace and schedule. Unless a teacher intervenes to mediate between the two realities—the reality of the school's demands and that of the student's makeup—it is the student who loses. It is a delicate balancing act and it goes on continuously. Yet, not even this kind of mediation is as difficult for a teacher as the one that follows.

The Teacher as Intervention Strategist

We had always been vaguely aware of Robbie. He was 15 and his tall, muscular presence made him impossible to ignore. But there was something else about him that drew our attention, something lurking and sinister. Robbie was one of those adolescents who had obvious problems in school and who simmered with hostility. Whether or not one factor caused the other, we were not sure. But we did know that he could hate! Usually without focus, but always with vigour.

His profile sharpened considerably one October morning when, apparently unprovoked, he set upon two boys in his class and beat them severely. A week later, he systematically destroyed a set of lockers and was only stopped when two teachers and a caretaker pinned him to the floor.

Robbie obviously needed help, but where to turn? He had already run the gamut of special services the school had to offer. The members of his family were no help; in fact, they were part of his problem. Unless something was done, Robbie was slated for expulsion.

His history teacher offered what became the solution.

Robbie was given the choice of withdrawing from school or of coming each day at 8:15 a.m.—not to sit idly or to satisfy some detention scheme, thereby heating up the hostility pattern—but to talk. The idea was that Robbie would talk out his frustration and anger with an adult who would listen—his history teacher. It was the simplest of therapies and it was totally successful.

The initial objective was solely to have Robbie defused before the school day began. But before long, Robbie was submitting to tutoring in his weak subjects. Even his chronic truancy decreased. Robbie, by the end of the year, was a dramatically changed young man. A tribute to those things that teachers accomplish before nine a.m.

It would be naive to think that all the Robbies are rescued so easily and so completely. Yet, the fact is that many of them are, not usually through such a formal arrangement as was necessary in Robbie's case, but not all students are as obviously in need of help as he was.

With every learning problem there is frustration. And that frustration takes so many forms. Sometimes, as in Robbie's case, it is explosive. Other students cover themselves with a veneer of sullenness which, unless penetrated by a teacher, protects them from the reality of their low achievement until they fade right out of the system. Some play the vacuous role which runs in varying degrees from a very loud "I-am-so-damn-dumb-there-isn't-a-thing-I-can't-screw-up-so-leave-me-alone" to the syndrome which combines an uncomprehending wide-eyed stare, shoulders that droop permanently at the bottom of a shrug, and bewildered muteness. Then, of course, there are the class clowns, the constant truants, and those who just dig in their heels in a metaphorical but unmistakeable "*NO!*" All these students need an advocate, a sympathetic listener, a mediator. But what they need most of all is someone with the courage to intervene.

Especially for adolescents, such a person is inevitably a teacher. This is partly because an adolescent seems to want a parent surrogate; partly it is because his needs become more apparent in school; and to be honest, it is partly because the teacher is simply there. Intervention of this type is certainly one of the most exciting but, equally, one of the most delicate and difficult tasks a teacher can perform. When, for example, should one intervene? And how? Even more difficult, is there a moral or ethical right to intervene at all? And, if one is satisfied with the reasoning that the context of "school" not only gives the right but makes it a responsibility, then to what extent does one intervene? Every student, in need of the kind of intervention a teacher can provide, trails behind him a conglomeration of influences: family, culture, socio-economic background, value system. Not only must teachers decide *when, how,* and *whether,* they must also determine the degree to which the student's problems are a matter of innate ability or of external forces. All this, while dealing with the frustration and the surface behaviours that both grow from and help to cause the student's learning problems.

Once in a while, teachers make mistakes in their intervention decision. Sometimes, mistakes are made because an active, fully-occupied classroom teacher does not have the time to mull over and figuratively weigh each ball before it is tossed into the air. The potential for error becomes very high when a teacher is trying to maintain, simultaneously, an individual relationship with up to thirty or forty people.

Usually, however, teachers' decisions to intervene are correct and effective. There are many reasons for this. One may be the simple fact that the teacher is the only one who is at the heart of the situation. Often, it is only the teacher who grasps both the student's perspective and that of the rest of the world. There is also the fact that, in the chain of those who make command decisions in education, it is only the teacher who is openly permitted some intuition, that sense of what is "right" for a student. And then there is the oft-forgotten point that schooling is a human process, designed to nurture the development and improvement of human personalities. Moving up and across the educational hierarchy usually means moving further and further away from the humanity of the student. A principal or headmaster is tugged by responsibilities to the system, the community, the demands of a large operation. A psychometrist sees sub-standard test results. A consultant inevitably lacks intimate knowledge of a case. If anyone is going to intervene with a troubled student, it is almost certainly a teacher.

Happily, there are times when the responsibility of intervening is not quite so awesome.

The Teacher as Mediator

One of my first principals, and one of my best, was a man with humour, great experience, and a chronic case of sinus. He was at retirement age and Jake, as we fondly referred to him, had developed those inevitable quirks of manner and character that are normal in aging but seem more pronounced in teachers, possibly because we are always under scrutiny.

Jake loved the loudspeaker system, and making school-wide announcements was his sole and exclusive prerogative. The morning recitation of The Lord's Prayer was his particular pride. Each day brought a new and definitive reading: sometimes mellifluous, sometimes sombre, occasionally measured, but always dramatic.

But his sinus condition caused problems. Jake could not

complete a sentence without a honk, cough, hack, snort, or other nasal recitative that would lift our students from their seats in a visible shudder. No one in our school slept through The Lord's Prayer.

Two boys in one of my ninth grade classes detected a pattern in Jake's proclivity. On warm, sunny days, they noted that Jake would lay out a mild cough. Cloudiness, increased humidity, and a bit of wind would generally cause a hacking harrumph. But in muggy, high-humidity weather, Jake really cleared the channels!

Billy and Ted began to collect data. For three months, they kept a daily chart of the temperature, humidity reading, wind velocity, etc., and cross-referenced this information with Jake's level of blowout. Then they took the results to their math teacher, gleefully confided their intent, and got her to help them interpret probability.

A week later, Billy and Ted opened underground pari-mutuel "windows". Students could bet five, ten, or twenty-five cents on the likelihood that morning of a cough, hack, or snort before "Give us this day our daily bread"!

The two boys made over three hundred dollars before their little enterprise was dissolved, but the story really doesn't end there. In a sense, it only began at that point.

Billy and Ted were students with learning difficulties. Their elementary school achievement records were dismal and they had been recipients of a number of "social promotions". When they arrived at high school, they were placed in one of those programmes that school systems loftily describe as "adjusted to meet special needs". At the time, these programmes were referred to in Ontario as "terminal"—from the death vocabulary of medicine!

When Jake learned of the betting operation, for it soon grew to unconcealable proportions, he was more pleased that it was conceived and managed by "terminals" than he was irritated by its existence. But, of course, it had to be stopped.

One morning, just before Lord's Prayer time, Jake suddenly appeared in front of Billy and Ted as they were tallying the previous day's payoffs.

"Here." Jake tried to look stern. "Put ten cents on a snort. I've got a cold this morning!"

The boys' bookmaking affair came to a thudding halt that day but without rancour, anger or the need for severe disciplinary measures. Naturally, Jake had to invoke his authority; schools are not intended to be betting shops. But he was a fine teacher and he left the door open for

Billy and Ted. They were punished but not in a way that would drive an even deeper wedge between the boys and their potential for education.[1]

More importantly, Jake and the math teacher took a personal, intervening interest in the two boys. Their abilities had been illuminated by the complexity and the success of their betting operation and every effort was made to nurture those abilities. Both boys eventually transferred into the regular school programme.

"Terminal" terminology has fallen from grace today in the search for gentler labelling, but "terminal" students are still around and still in need of the special kind of treatment that Billy and Ted received.

So many students with learning problems are embittered by their failure and they soon learn to conceive of the world as an us-against-them situation. They act out against the system, deliberately transgressing its values and principles, and then, when they are caught and punished, regard that outcome as confirmation of their original perception. Teachers break this cycle. To these students, teachers are the most immediate representatives of the alien value system. But it is also teachers who are best able to lead these students to an understanding of these values and, hence, to the realization that difficulty in school is not necessarily the product of an adversary relationship. It is another facet of the teacher's role as mediator. What makes this particular aspect of the role so difficult is that the teacher, while in the process of attempting to break the cycle, must act simultaneously as enforcer of those very principles that the students associate with "them". A teacher's role would be easier if she were just an enforcer. It would be easier, too, if she were just a counsellor. But she is not. A teacher is both. The task is sensitive and difficult but there is no one else to do it. It's why the teacher is the key.

The Teacher and Technology

I prepared all summer for Class J-11-12. The reports promised it would be the biggest challenge ever. Twelve students ranging in age from thirteen to seventeen. Four girls, eight boys, with a mean reading level of 1.8 (6-7 years old), according to the G.D.R.A.[2] and the C.T.B.S.[3] The reports went on to suggest

---

[1]The boys were put in charge of the collection, tabulation, and storage of all the grade nine textbooks at the end of the school year—over two thousand books. Ted devised a system that, in modified form, the school still uses.

[2]The Group Diagnostic and Reading Aptitude Test. (Monroe M. and Sherman E.E. Nevins Printing, 1966) often referred to as the "old reliable". I have always felt it should be referred to as the "old, easy-to-administer, quick, and cheap", factors which must account at least in part for its frequent use.

[3]The Canadian Test of Basic Skills (Kind, E.M. et al., Nelson & Sons, 1974). In twenty years of involvement with "special" adolescents, I've never found a test with so little to merit its popularity.

that their teacher should operate on the assumption that they could not read at all.

On the first day of class, fourteen students showed up. One of the extras was Bryan, distinguished not by his size which was considerable, nor by his decibel-level which was even greater, but by the fact that he had a tattered paperback in his hip pocket. It was a pornographic novel: true, hard-core porn. One of the worst—or best—I've ever encountered!

And it went through J-11-12 in less than two weeks! Everyone read it. They had group readings in the cafeteria; they read it surreptitiously behind their textbooks; they read it balanced on their knees under the desk.

The book had no pictures, it was full-length, and the prose was a stilted translation from another language. A reading level formula—for what it is worth—placed the novel at approximately Grade 7.0—somewhat above the 1.8 mean of J-11-12. Yet everyone read it. And I know everyone read it because, out of an absolutely insatiable curiosity, I gave a comprehension test on it!

Eight months later, J-11-12 applied en masse to take driver education. A prerequisite is a written test, based on a manual of good driving practices and driving regulations. Thirteen of the fourteen[1] *wrote and passed on the first sitting. So much for the precision of J-11-12's psychometric evaluations.*

Early in the 1950's, the late American philosopher, Paul Goodman, lamented the increasing spread of "hardware disease", the absolute faith of western society in technology and the consequent intrusion of technology into areas where it has no place. Certainly Goodman must have foreseen what was to happen to education, for technology has driven a wedge into that magic that happens when a teacher and student come together to grow and understand and learn.

This is not to argue against certain positive features that technology has given teachers. The development of audio-visual machinery and all its accompanying software—films, filmstrips, videotapes, audiotapes, and such things as the improvement of communication aids for the handicapped—have made the teacher's functional role easier and are a welcome addition to education. But these are aids; they are peripheral to the teaching-learning process, incidental to the relationship of a teacher and student. The damage is in the compelling ethos of technology, the use of a technological approach to what is essentially a human activity.

The teaching-learning process is necessarily an elastic, continuous,

[1]The failure was Bryan who was seventeen and already had a driver's licence!

constantly shifting thing that varies in intensity and thrives on flexibility, adjustment, and spontaneity. The technological approach, however, dictates that this process be reduced to something neat, static, and "bite-size". It dictates that the student be assessed, diagnosed, labelled, and stamped for programming; that the needs, thus determined, be met by expertly designed curriculum, administered in prescribed doses; and that the teacher arrange and apply that curriculum strictly on the basis of measurable criteria. In its pure, theoretical form, the approach is unassailable. And its appeal is irresistible—to behaviourists, management consultants, and robots!

For students who are generally successful in school, technology or non-technology is of little consequence, for they are either able enough to ignore what they choose or willing enough to play whatever new game is set before them. The damage for students with difficulties is profound because, for them, technology is regarded as a saviour.

These students have always been a challenge for teachers, and to seek help with them seems a fairly natural inclination. But seeking this help through the technological approach simply imposes even heavier doses of those factors that intensify learning problems: fragmentation, unyielding precision, insistence on limits of time, bigness, rigidity, the exclusion of intuition, and worst of all—numbers.

Numbers are the means by which modern education joins the realm of "mysterious science". Just as the equipment in a medical doctor's office gives hint of strange and esoteric knowledge, shared only by the select, just as lawyers' offices are lined with imposing tomes and their speech filled with conditionals and subjunctives, so numbers are the smokescreen of mystery in education. Regrettably, they are also a curse on the relationship between the teacher and a student with learning problems.

To begin with, there is the I.Q. test, a still popular instrument despite overwhelming evidence of its inaccuracy. Then there is the achievement test, the diagnostic test, the abilities test, all producing numbers which baffle parents, label students, and undermine teaching. Even much of the curriculum for the slower learning student is reduced by formula to the "appropriate grade level".

One of the most dangerous outcomes of these numbers is their prophetic self-fulfillment. A poor test result for a student with learning problems becomes, not an explanation of his problem, but a confirmation of it to his disappointed parents, a further erosion of the student's self-image, a justification for the school's programme for him, and a roadblock for the teacher. It works this way. The classroom teacher, who, more than anyone else, is in a position to see potential in a student far above that which was measured, is blocked by the imposing authority of that test result. ("After all Ms ________, the test does have a validity coefficient of .87 and a reliability coefficient of .73. Surely you . . .") Most often, the teacher is not a technician, is not equipped for statistical argument, and caves in. The outcome for the student follows a time-honoured script: his results were low; he must be low; so treat him as low. Then, as the object of low expectation and the recipient of low challenge, the student performs at a low level. The prophecy is fulfilled. ("See! The test was right!")

Only when the teacher is given more credibility than the technology is this self-fulfilling prophecy interrupted. The teacher is the only one, in the chain of those responsible for this student, who has access to more than the technological data. The teacher is the only one with access to that student's pace and rhythm, fears and preferences, defences and mannerisms—all of which have a profound effect on achievement, but none of which can be tapped by technology. To rely entirely on technology heightens the potential for misdiagnosis, incorrect placement, and inappropriate programming. It is simply not possible to reduce the needs of an exceptional student to a series of precise and measurable but fragmented and sterile objectives. Technology can help this student, but only if it is controlled by a sensitive teacher who combines it with understanding, intuition, and, above all, common sense. Teaching and learning are dynamic human endeavours and they will always be so.

Teaching Is The Most Exciting Thing You Can Do With Your Clothes On

After three years in the classroom I was no longer a novice. And since that time had been spent almost exclusively with the "special" classes, I should have known better. But . . .

It was a week before March vacation—the silly season. The class before me was 9F. They were to be followed by 9J and 9M—three all-male groups known as The Triumvirate, the degree of whose collective hyperkinesis was in inverse ratio to their alphabetical order. Yet, on this particular morning, 9F's behaviour was exemplary. To begin with, everyone walked into class and went directly to his seat. No trip-ups, U.F.O.'s, booby traps, or door-jamming. Also, everyone had homework done. No carbons, no photocopies, no arms in slings, no excuses.

And their responses were remarkable. They answered with insight, in complete sentences, and with no slang. To my every question every hand went up. Several of them even stood up to answer! Something was afoot, but I hadn't the faintest idea what. There were no visitors in the room and I was not being inspected—occasions when the boys always came through. There had been no promise of early dismissal, no solicitation of favours, and they knew the vice-principal had pneumonia!

I couldn't stand it. "OK, what's going on?" Silence. However, a lot of eye-movement told me I'd struck a chord.

"Who is the show for?"

Still nothing.

"Look! I'm not upset. It's my curiosity that's killing me!"

Slowly the response came.

"You ask him."

"No, you ask him!"

"You!"

"WELL, SOMEBODY ASK ME!"

Long pause.

"It's Rebelski, sir."

That was it! Piggy Rebelski was the creative genius, the capo of capos and the class clown of 9J.

"If it's Rebelski, I don't want to know anything about it. Let's get back to the lesson."

"Oh, but you've gotta, sir!"

"Yeah! You gotta!"

"I gotta what?"

The silence this time was shorter, but absolute.

"We want to go to gym, sir."

"Why? 9J's in gym now. You don't get gym till next period!"

"Yeah, sir, we wanna go to the dressing room now, sir. Can you let us out?"

"Whatever for?"

"Well sir, cause . . . cause . . . cause Piggy Rebelski's gonna torch a fart!"

Piggy was a blazing technicolour success. So much so that his shorts caught fire, set off an automatic alarm, and brought a platoon of fire trucks to the school. A concentration of all the creative power in our school system could not have predicted such an event that morning, and *that,* among many other things, is what makes teaching so exciting. Dull moments are rare. Often the fun is unintended, as on the day when one of my most terribly serious students began his oral-presentation biography thus: "*Elizabeth I was known as the virgin queen. As a queen she was a real success.*" Sometimes it is deliberate: never more so than when a student catches a teacher. After several months of haranguing my students about ambiguity, I foolishly offered the following question on a brief test: "Give the export of coal from Nova Scotia for any one year." One of my sharper students responded: "1492: none".

However, the excitement of teaching is not just in the repartee and wit, the irony and burlesque. There is even more excitement in working with young people and watching them grow and understand and learn, especially if they have learning problems. Burgess, at the time of writing, is a watchmaker. Molly is a hairdresser. Piggy, now known as Vince, is a car salesman. Virginia is in her third year of remission, a very positive sign. Bryan lost an election bid to become a trustee on his local board of education. Robbie owns a small catering service. Billy makes a comfortable living betting on horse races and Ted owns a hardware store.

To believe that one has had a positive influence in the life of another is the reward of teaching. It is this belief that stimulates, that provides the impetus for a teacher to be an active mediator, a facilitator, a manipulator of time and environment. It supports the faith that something can be done to help the student who is slow, afraid, misdirected, confused, or disabled. Teachers affect eternity for no one knows where their influence ends.

CHAPTER 2

WHY ARE THEY THAT WAY?

THERE IS A strange kind of comfort in knowing the cause of a student's learning problem. There is comfort for the student, since the clear establishment of cause relieves him of some of the responsibility for his poor performance in school. There is comfort for the teacher, since knowing the cause explains, at least in part, why the student's progress is often so painfully slow despite massive efforts to effect change. "Searching for cause" is an intellectual process that goes to the very roots of our culture. It explains why parents so frequently turn to medical doctors when it becomes apparent that their child is experiencing learning difficulties. It explains why, in the early days of special education, teachers turned so readily toward a medical model for guidance in the remediation of learning problems. There persisted then, and still does for some, a fond hope that somewhere in the technology of science was a means of specifically diagnosing all the causes and, therefore, a specific cure for each of them. Would that it were so, that it were that simple!

The forces that produce a learning problem are so varied and complex, so elusive and limitless, that it is impossible to refine them into specific descriptions. In fact, to be strictly empirical, one must confine a discussion of causes to general observations rather than attempt a specific delineation. Observations like:

(a) Learning problems generated by a single, easily identified cause are probably the least frequent type a teacher will encounter.
(b) By the time the existence of a learning problem is clearly established to all concerned, what may once have been the cause has usually been interwoven with and compounded by a series of other factors. This is especially the case with an adolescent.
(c) The older the person with a learning problem, the more difficult the correction of the problem will be.
(d) Even knowing a cause does not imply a remedy.

These are among the very few observations about causes on which both practitioners and theoreticians agree. Ultimately, a discussion of the *why* of learning problems is necessarily subject to the arbitrary choice of whoever is leading the discussion. The list of causes suggested by the case studies in this chapter stems from the author's twenty years of practical experience. It would be presumptuous to pretend that it is definitive.

Genetic Causes

This is Stuart, 12 years old. He is writing instructions for walking from our school to his home.

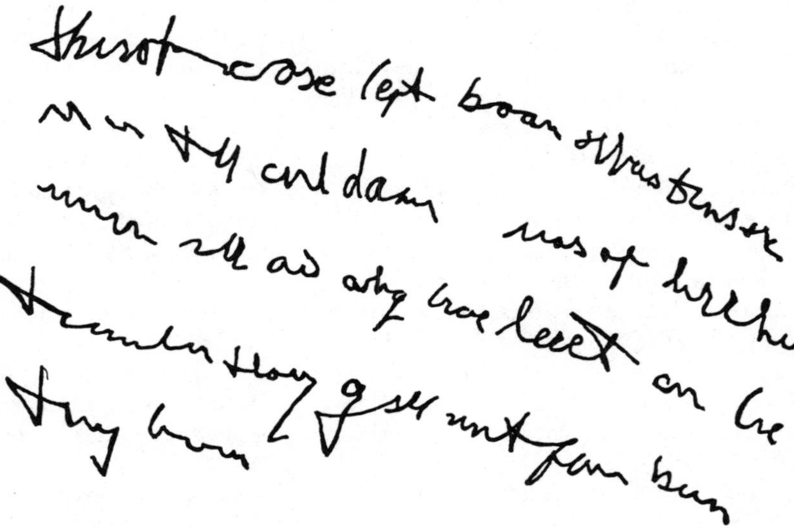

Probably Stuart had a learning disability—a *genuine* learning disability—for never was a useful term more abused or misapplied. Stuart, when he wrote those instructions, knew exactly what he wanted to write, and what you see above represents his best effort to do so. Stuart could not process the words in his head into a written form that others could read. Our consultant at the time called it dysgraphia. Probably she was right. Since he had great difficulty reading, Stuart no doubt had dyslexia as well. Not that he was to be mired forever at this level. On the opposite page is Stuart, two tedious and hard working years later.

For the Stuarts of the world, the future is not necessarily bleak. Because his teachers were willing to try and because Stuart was willing to try, his reading and writing improved. But what of the cause? Why did Stuart write like that? If he had a learning disability, and both common sense and all the expertise we could muster indicated that indeed he had, then it was likely he was born with it. His younger sister and still

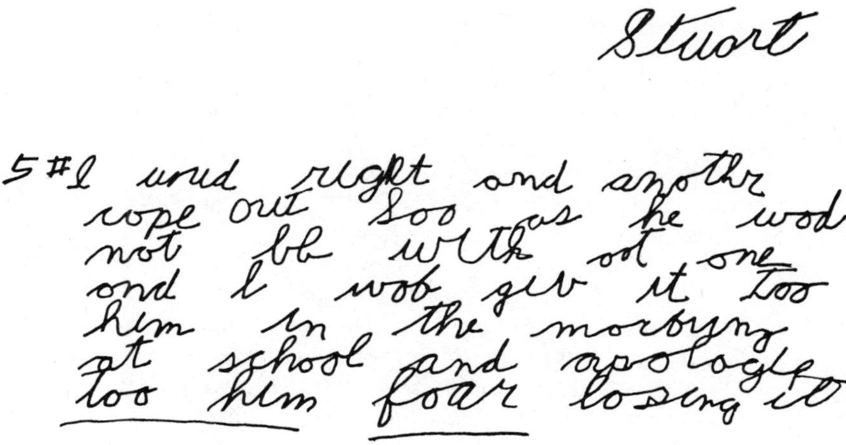
Stuart
5 #I wrud right and anothr
rope out soo as he wod
not bb with ot one
and I wob giv it too
him in the morbyng
at school and apologe
too him foar losing it

younger brother showed similar disabilities of varying degree. Likely they, too, were born that way.

Most theories that attempt to explain learning disabilities ultimately agree that a genuine learning disability is the result of some flaw in the central nervous system. What this means to the student and to the teacher is that feeling of strange comfort mentioned at the beginning of this chapter. At least, once the presence of a learning disability or any other genetic flaw is established, then the student's poor performance is no one's fault. It is a base from which to begin. A physically handicapped person may admit to playing basketball poorly without loss of peer status or self-image or teacher-understanding. In the same sense, a person with a genetically based learning problem may admit to the reality of poor academic performance and, from that base, work toward better things. For the teacher, such knowledge may not necessarily change the amount of work to be done or even the pedagogy to be used, but certainly it will affect the way he views that student.

Traumatic Causes

The difference between learning problems that are genetically based and those which are caused by trauma, that is, physical injury, is frequently a matter of drama. Take the case of Phil.

> *Like most 17 year olds, Phil saw graduation from grade 12 as a good reason for a party. And why not? He had passed with honours. So had his girlfriend. The long warm days of summer were ahead. He had a great summer job, and all his friends were returning to school with him in the fall. There was nothing but sunshine in his future.*

Of course, the party was great. A little too much booze perhaps, and maybe they shouldn't have thrown the girls into the pool with their new dresses and all, but what the heck!

At 4 a.m. Phil piled the family Volkswagen into the side of a bridge. He was in a coma for just over a year and then awoke to a wheelchair, paralysis on the right side, elliptical speech, and haphazard memory. His left occipital lobe had been damaged.

When Phil came to us three years later, he had recovered some mobility but still had very limited speech. He could recognize many words and comprehend short passages of prose on familiar subjects but could not recite the alphabet or repeat new words after a ten-second interlude. He could do some analytical geometry but had difficulty writing the numbers from 1 - 10.

We really didn't know what to do with Phil.

No great insight was necessary to comprehend Phil's learning problem. It was dramatically and tragically obvious—the cause was simple to determine. It was also a striking example of a case where knowledge of the cause was of limited help. Yet not a single teacher turned away from Phil. Although none of us had anything but the vaguest notion of what might help him, we all tried, relying basically on two of teaching's strongest weapons: instinct and patience. Phil began to show gradual improvement. More speech, more movement, more awareness, more memory. And, at the time of writing, he continues to do so.

Whether Phil is improving because of teaching or because of some natural recovery process, we do not know. However, it is reasonable to believe that the atmosphere of learning and stimulation created for him is a significant factor. At least, the creation of such an atmosphere is positive and progressive and useful—an effective antidote for the all too prevalent attitude that conditions like Phil's automatically imply a learning "ceiling", a terminal learning capacity.

Herein, of course, lies one of the dangers in the search for cause, particularly for the genetic/traumatic cases: the assumption that, because the cause is organic, the potential for improvement has a limit. It is a curse from which the mentally retarded are constantly trying to escape and it applies just as strongly to people like Stuart and Phil. It may well be possible to identify the cause of certain learning problems, particularly when those problems have a physiological base, but no matter how much certainty there can be about the cause, there can never be absolute certainty about its effect. No one knows how far these students can go.

Behavioural Causes

There is no question that Libby, aged 12, had a learning problem.

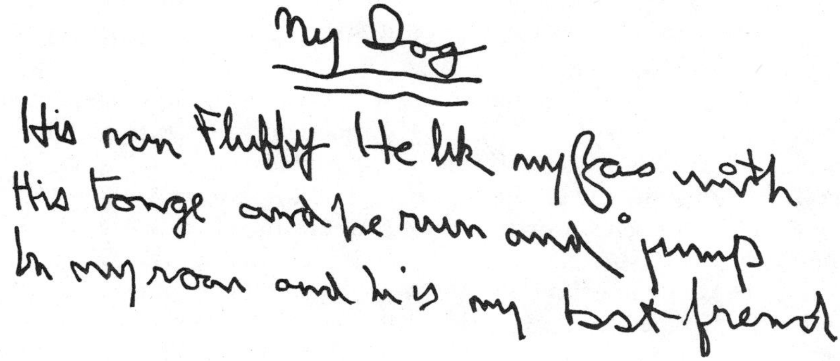
My Dog
His nam Fluffy He lik my fas with
His tonge and he run and jump
In my roon and hi's my bst frend

But then so did Sergio.

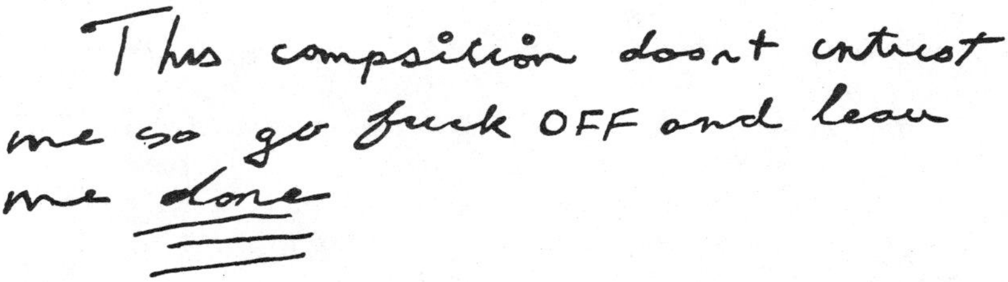
This compsicion doont intrest
me so go fuck OFF and leau
me done

Sergio was a husky, brooding, 15 year old who carried his frustrations like a shield of defiance. Every teacher of adolescents has at least one Sergio every year: the kind of student who does not learn with ease, yet is not the weakest in the group; the kind who does not cause difficulty very often, yet when his advice is to "fuck off", it seems discreet to do so. Sergio was classified in our school as a behavioural student. In other words, his primary problem was behaviour, but implicit in that diagnosis are problems in learning as well.

With Sergio and other "behavioural" students like him, one of the real conundrums is the matter of cause and effect. Did Sergio become a behaviour problem because he *had* a learning problem or did his behaviour cause him to fall so far behind in his school progress that he *developed* a learning problem? To know the root cause would be helpful to a teacher, for then it might be possible to deal with the elements that cause the counter-productive behaviour or to treat the learning problem. But Sergio was an adolescent, and the root cause was buried somewhere in his personal history, covered over so deeply with defences, reactions, and hostilities, that not even he could figure out where the source of his problem lay. Sergio conducted himself in a way which forced us to deal *first* with his behaviour. Yet, we also knew that he had, whatever the cause, a learning problem.

A teacher must deal with both matters. It is not enough to deal with behaviour alone; for there to be any permanent impact, the learning problems must be met too. A fine balancing act for the teacher, yet an act that few others but the teacher are equipped to perform.

Problems in behaviour are certainly not limited to the Sergio types. There are those students whose presentation of self is so counter-productive that remediation of learning problems becomes a remote dream. The immediate need to deal with the surface behaviours makes learning a secondary objective. Then there are those who occupy the completely opposite end of the scale, students like Timmy.

By one of those quirks in a system that simply does not provide adequately for many of its "special" students, Timmy ended up in my behavioural class because "There's no other place for him." He was 14, very small, and asthmatic. His voice, when he had the courage to use it, squeaked embarrassingly. He was inept in academics and clumsy at sports, not because he was naturally poor at either but because he was so terrified of everything. He was terrified of failure; he was terrified of success. He was afraid of his classmates and he was afraid of me. Timmy lived in the belief that his world was out to get him. Unfortunately, his world did much to oblige.

Like Sergio, Timmy had a behaviour problem and a learning problem. Although there were sharp contrasts in personality, what the two boys had in common was fear: fear of the effort, the failure, the awareness, the delight, and the shock that come with learning. Where they differed was in their manner of meeting that fear. Timmy shrank from it and Sergio defied it. In the process, they shrank from and defied, respectively, everything associated with the learning process: the school, their teacher, their classmates.

Whether the behaviour is a cause or an effect is uncertain. What is certain is that, by adolescence, this behaviour has become a barricade behind which these students hide. Unless a teacher intervenes, their chances of realizing their potential may be limited.

Cultural/Environmental Causes

When I first met Elvie she was 15 and had already spent several years in a special all-girl class. She was not really exceptional in an intellectual sense nor could she have even been termed "difficult to manage". Elvie was optimistic, cheerful, kind, and patient. But she was utterly lacking in any of those social niceties and patterns of behaviour to which most of our society pay at least nominal attention. Elvie never deliberately embarrassed anyone; it just seemed to happen that way. Nor was she deliberately unhygienic. Hygiene just didn't matter. Several other girls in the class had braces on their teeth and rarely opened their mouths without first putting up their hands as a screen. Elvie had almost no teeth, a fact which she unabashedly and constantly revealed with her wide-open smile.

The morning on which Elvie became firmly locked in my memory began ordinarily enough, until one of the class had an epileptic seizure. After the immediate situation passed, I set my lesson aside to allow the girls to talk out their excitement. The talk inevitably turned to incidents such as the one we had just witnessed. Instead of calming down, the girls became more stirred up with tales of emergency medical experiences—each tale wilder than the one before. Through it all, Elvie sat calmly and quietly as she normally did. But the need to contribute was too powerful.

She sat up on her desk. "Hey sir!" (Elvie prefaced everything with 'Hey!', and never spoke without either sitting on the desk or putting her foot on the seat.)

"When I started the men - menistrate - y'know, your period? My mother took me to this here gin - gin . . ."

"Gynecologist, Elvie, gynecologist", I blurted, red-faced, groping through my mind for a way to change the subject.

"Yeah, that's it. Gynecologist. And d'y'know what he did?" She grabbed the hem of her skirt, leaned back on the desk and was about to demonstrate the gynecological examination when there occurred one of those events that convinces one there is a God and that He looks after teachers. The fire-bell rang! Never before or since in my career have I abandoned a classroom as quickly![1]

[1]It would be unfair to Elvie to leave the postscript untold. Shortly after this incident, a new teacher was added to the staff to teach grooming, hygiene, and life-skills. Her success with Elvie was considerable. Nor does the story end there. As part of a community work-skills programme, we involved this class with a day-care nursery, a senior citizens' home, and a chronic care hospital. Elvie turned out to be gifted in dealing with old people. It seemed that there wasn't a single geriatric patient, no matter how difficult, ill, or cantankerous, who did not submit to Elvie's patient cheerfulness. For the latter part of the school year, Elvie enjoyed great peer status for she had been offered a position immediately upon graduation. At the time of this writing, she is a nursing assistant in a senior citizens' home.

One of the first things a teacher learns in his rookie year is that, from time to time, he will meet students who have been raised in value systems different from his own and often significantly at variance with the social norms to which most schools subscribe. There may indeed be a validity, an integrity to these systems, but they are different. A student from such a system often seems to have learning problems or, perhaps more accurately, achievement problems. Certainly, one could not label Elvie as retarded or stupid. Yet, her performance in the traditional academic sense was indeed retarded, but not for lack of intellect. Elvie just did not find school all that important. She cared little for precision, paid limited attention to "correctness", and was certainly unaggressive—all qualities that reduce one's chances in the game of school.

Elvie's potentially embarrassing behaviour in the "gynecologist incident" was certainly not deliberate. To talk in abstract descriptive terms, to find euphemisms, to avoid reality for the sake of social grace was simply not part of her make-up. In Elvie's terms, if one described a visit to the gynecologist, one demonstrated what transpired during the examination. Whether or not such a profile constitutes a learning problem often depends upon whose point of view is accepted. Unfortunately for Elvie and all students like her, the accepted point of view is rarely theirs.

Nevertheless, their situation in school must be viewed empirically: if students like these are not succeeding in school, the fact must be recognized and dealt with. What constitutes the challenge for the classroom teacher is to expose these students to the demands of the society's dominant value system, without implying dishonour to their own.

With students like Elvie the challenge is not overwhelming, for it is reasonable to argue that Elvie's situation was more one of blithe unawareness than of active rejection. The situation that follows was considerably different.

Watford and Woneena were black West Indians. They were twins, aged 14, and had come from Jamaica to Canada two years before. There was a large minority of black West Indians in the school and the twins were leaders.

Although both of them were potentially able students, neither of them came even remotely close to success. Watford deliberately affected the behaviour and accent of the American urban black, stereotyped on television programmes. He never walked; he danced from place to place to music that seemed to play in his head whenever his eyes were closed. His only response, when addressed by a teacher, was "What for?" which he pronounced "Whafoah?"

Woneena's mouth, however, was always open. She led a coterie of five or six girls who chattered, and giggled, and bounced around incessantly. They were never still or quiet.

Neither twin ever completed assignments; they didn't even bring books or pens to class. They left the impression that they were totally outside of the school environment even though they were present in it. They weren't even on the periphery. The twins and their friends had created a world of their own.

Both Watford and Woneena had learning problems. In some taxonomies of cause they might be included under the "behaviour" category. Yet, it was clear that their learning and their behaviour problems were part of a cultural and environmental issue. In many ways, these young people were the end result of a variety of influences not of their own making. They lived with their parents in state-supported housing—literally a ghetto of people like themselves—where the kind of behaviour they exhibited in school went unnoticed. Their parents were unskilled labourers who had never been to school, so there was little role-model impetus for the twins to succeed. Even the school system militated against them in an ironic way. Because the West Indians were a minority, they could perceive themselves as different from the dominant culture in the school. Yet, because the minority was a large one, there was sufficient strength and reactionary peer pressure to set up a subculture. Within the school, they literally carried on as a separate unit with its own codes and values. The result was a kind of group-enforced school failure. Even if Watford and Woneena had wanted to change, it is entirely possible that they would have been prevented from doing so. Here was a learning problem born of cultural confusion and conflict.

Sometimes, the cultural conflicts are not so broadly generalized yet still cause learning difficulties. There are many students who emigrate from different cultures and who actively attempt to integrate with the dominant culture but have learning problems because of language barriers. Others find it nearly impossible to understand the cognitive styles of the dominant culture. Some find it difficult to accept or even comprehend the dominant behaviour patterns. All these students, the Elvies, the Watfords and Woneenas, are caught in a no-man's land. They are not fully part of the prevailing culture, yet they can neither ignore nor reject it because what they bring from their own systems is not strong enough or helpful enough. They need the help of their teachers.

Uncertain Causes

This is the largest group of all. Despite the research, the theorizing, the assessing, and the diagnosing, the reality for the classroom teacher is that one can rarely be absolutely certain *why* an adolescent has a learning difficulty. There can be educated guesses and, of course, there are assumptions. There are the questionable data of standardized tests. But, ultimately, the majority of adolescents do not fit neatly on any one shelf of a taxonomy of causes. The problems are too complex and their roots too obscure. How is it possible, for example, to really explain Renate's writing in the following samples?

She wrote this one morning during a regular writing period.

hide they whore farsts run and
they Soct the fursts rign and the
rangr dzrgd and the most put
the a shoz in a canter and
dron them the thy sew my.
and I ran and thy sole toj.
my but I tuey a roke.
ta ane af they and thy
weriy stit shoting at my
and I ran in the cave.
and thy were wtci they. thet
one of them came in
cave but I kill thm.

She wrote this directly after lunch on the same day!

digging in the garden after
dusk turnupall sort of surprize
first you needa good strong light...

Renate was entirely unpredictable, not only in performance but also in behaviour. A psychiatrist told us she believed Renate might be schizophrenic but admitted, "I'm really not at all sure."

Or what of Anton? A strange situation indeed.

Anton was placed in my special class at the age of 12—two years early—at the request of a family court judge. He was a juvenile offender. He was the fourth of four sons in a family that emigrated from Europe. Five languages were spoken in the home. In Anton's file were the results of five different I.Q. tests, each of which showed him to be well below the borderline retarded level. Indeed, during my initial assessment of him, Anton could neither write nor recite the alphabet and he could not multiply beyond the 4 times table. Yet, every Saturday morning, with the express approval of his father, Anton bought a Racing Form, read it, made eight selections, and placed bets with a local bookie. His success, while not extraordinary, was enough to give him more cash than the older boys in the class. Was Anton just too smart for the system?

Here is a piece of writing from Robin. At 12, he could not write or recite the alphabet either.

<u>the murder in the alley</u>
one day I had a Phone
Call it was mr. carlson the
captiun of the police depart-ment
He told me to hurry over becuse
There was a died body so I
Rushed over There and he said
I want you to go in the apartment
because Thats were he got killed
go go check some prints in the
Apartment so I went up there
and the door was locked. I wonderd
why so I started to bust The
door down and I seen blood
all over the floor I tasted The
blood and it was [redacted] fake blood

Perhaps one of the most typical of the "uncertain cause" learning problems was Morty. If anything, he was a conglomerate of causes.

From the point of view of a typical 17 year old, Morty was outstanding for all the wrong reasons, but then Morty was not typical. He was unwashed and unkempt. His clothes didn't fit. His hair, which never saw comb or brush, would invariably telegraph how well and on what side he had slept the night before. His shoes were never tied.

But it was his eyes that really distinguished Morty. The eyes were wide and protruding, suggesting a possible thyroid condition. And one eye wandered. When he was angry with us—which was often—he would fix us with an indignant

> *glare. But the whole composure would collapse as his left eye drifted off north by north east.*
>
> *Morty looked slow; he sounded slow; his movements were slow. And, for six years, he attended a school for the retarded. Yet, after this, in another school, Morty learned to read. Here, he organized and administered school dances. Still, he seemed almost to resist learning. What he was taught one day would seem to be entirely gone the next.*
>
> *All this was compounded by Morty's reaction to people who laughed at him. He played the clown and made himself seem even slower than he was.*

Morty's problem, it seemed, was related to a whole list of causes: genetic, environmental, behavioural, perhaps cultural, maybe traumatic—and most definitely, *uncertain.*

To find the very core of Morty's problem had become impossible by the time he was seventeen years of age. Maybe it all began because of the poverty of his family and the life style they followed. Or was it because he looked strange, thereby causing people to lower their expectations of him? Was the cause educational? Did placement in a school for retarded children allow Morty to function below his capacity? Perhaps it was genetic? Did he have the kind of episodic memory that some learning disabled people have? More likely, it was a combination of all these causes, as well as some others we don't even know about.

Even had we known the primary cause of Morty's problem, there is good reason to doubt that the information would have been of much value. As with most adolescents with learning difficulties, Morty was a product of the primary cause or causes. Over time, he had become hardened to the reality of his supposed deficiencies and had learned the defences, the avoidance behaviours, and the circumvention strategies necessary to deal with them. By the time of adolescence, primary causes were too remote to remediate. In this sense, Morty was like so many of his colleagues. Unlike "normal" adolescents, who presumably are in a state of developmental flux throughout this period, adolescents with learning problems tend to be more rigid in personality, more difficult to change.

Yet within the problem lies the hope. While Morty and all those young people like him are drawing the battle lines, they are also developing strengths. At worst, these strengths are mere survival skills; at best, they are techniques of coping and adopting and substituting. Through experience, by being in school, by inter-relating with other people, and by virtue of their own inherent and untapped abilities, these adolescents develop a range of talents and aptitudes and expertise. They have potential. What is needed is someone to unlock that potential. What they need is a key.

CHAPTER 3
WHAT HAPPENS BECAUSE THEY ARE THAT WAY?

I FIRST SAW the following "conversation", written on the top of a desk, in a classroom for slower students. Obviously, the "conversation" between the two students who shared this desk required several days to complete. The fact that it was allowed to continue without being scrubbed away was a tribute to the good sense and good humour of both the teacher and the janitorial staff.

DIE! DIE! MY DARLING

WHY? WHY? MY LOVE!

BECAUSE! BECAUSE! MY FOOL!

THATS SO? THATS SO? MY DEER?

WHO? WHO? MY MYSTERY?

A LOVER! A LOVER! MY SWEET!

A NAME! A NAME! MY LOVER!

LOOK HERE, BEFORE WE GO ANY FARTHER I WANT TO MAKE SURE WE DON'T GET SERIOUS OK?

DON'T WORRY. I WON'T GET SERIOUS. YOUR NAME! YOUR NAME! MY ADMIRER!

A. NONYMOUS! A. NONYMOUS! MY GUESSER!

WHAT PERIOD? WHAT PERIOD? MY NONYMOUS?

THE 8TH. THE 8TH. MY FRIEND.

I KNOW YOU! I KNOW YOU, MY COMRADE! (MARY HOOD?)

YES! YES! BUT WHO ARE YOU?

FIND OUT! FIND OUT! AND GOOD LUCK!

WHAT PERIOD? WHAT PERIOD? MY TORMENTOR?

FROM 1-9! FROM 1-9.

WHAT GRADE? WHAT GRADE? MY SMARTIE!

At this point, a third person got into the act.

Why don't you ever talk to me dear?

NOW LOOK! I'M TALKING TO MARY SO THE OTHER PERSON GET LOST!

YOU'RE NIEL! YOU'RE NIEL!

I'M NOT NIEL! I'M NOT NIEL!
DON'T LIE! YOU ARE! SO THERE!
I'M NEIL. NOT NIEL.
ALRIGHT. ALRIGHT. THAT'S IT!
THAT'S WHAT? MY MARY!
THE END. THE END. MY FOOL.

This could just as easily have been a "conversation" between ordinary students or even gifted students. But it wasn't. It was the interplay of two adolescents in a school for slower students. The conversation is charming; it is certainly amusing—to adults at least; and it is strikingly *normal.*

For the major part of their day-to-day lives, adolescents with learning difficulties are really no different from the rest of their peers. They face similar problems, similar challenges, have similar needs and wants. Like other adolescents, they have desires and disappointments, loves and hates, opinions and beliefs. And they deal with these elements of their lives in very similar ways. In short, the learning-problem adolescent, in just about every way, is the same as every other adolescent. *Outside school.*

The President's Committee on Mental Retardation (1970), in the U.S.A., described it best. The "six-hour" mentally retarded was the term they used. In other words, these students function well before 9 a.m. and after 3 p.m. Very few teachers would dispute this. The adolescent who has enormous difficulties reading and writing can often be seen completing a complicated service order at some car repair shop after school. Or the one who has difficulties wading through the complexities of fractions, percentages, and decimals can often be seen, on Saturday, deftly fingering a cash register in a supermarket. Or what of the irresponsible student who never brings books, who never has work completed, but who leaves school at 3 p.m. to take charge of a range of younger siblings because both parents work the graveyard shift (4 p.m. - midnight)?

Life is not an extra-curricular activity. Clearly, these students do have resources which indicate a potential for success. And these resources, most of the time, extend beyond mere "coping skills". Yet the striking—and depressing—reality is that the resources surface so rarely in school. The fact that these students are generally unsuccessful between 9 a.m. and 3 p.m. is not the product of someone's imagination. Most of them are indeed performing poorly.

What makes them so different from other adolescents in a learning situation? What makes them so different for the six hours of a school day? The chart that follows is a starting point in determining why.

Adolescents with Learning Problems: Characteristics and their Outcome

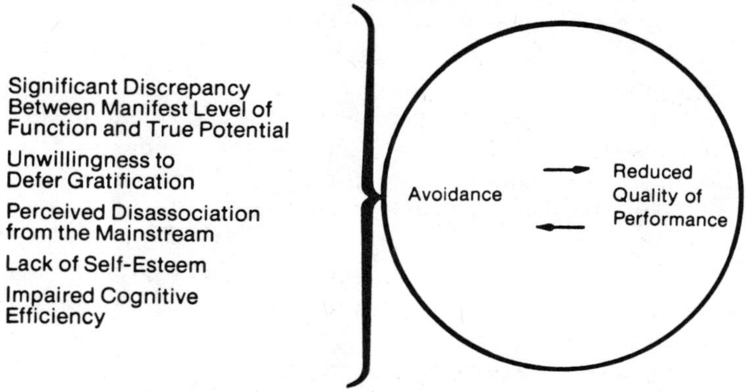

Significant Discrepancy between Manifest Level of Function and True Potential

Vanda, aged 13, wrote the following two pieces on consecutive school days. The first was written as part of a regular, organized, and structured writing programme.

Being A Lady

Being a lady is very important when you are around anybody. When people are talking you don't but in. When you sit down don't slam yourself down, sit down as if you are a ballet dancer. Don't sit at the table or any other place biting your nails. Also when you receive something you should always use your manners (no matter where you are you should always use your manners.) Be polite where ever you are too be.

On the next day, Vanda wrote the following as part of an exercise in writing sentences to demonstrate the meaning of words.

1. *The lady wear a casual dreess.*
2. *Charcoal is your in the barbecue.*
3. *The manoger has a big responsability in the store.*
4. *We use stov the cook to food.*
5. *The gils supper is extermely.*
6. *The hen and the roster got togather and had a fertil egg.*

Although Vanda's first piece of writing does not imply a destiny as a writer, it is clearly superior to the second collection of sentences. Yet both efforts were made on consecutive days by the same student. Vanda reveals two levels of writing ability, one of which is measurably better than the other. The implications are several—and significant. The most obvious is the point that Vanda is not consistent in the level of ability she demonstrates. All too frequently the level that her teachers saw and were asked to evaluate was below the level of which she was truly capable. This is typical of all adolescents with problems. With distressing regularity they fail to reveal their true potential.

Much of this has to do with the perception these adolescents have of a task and the consequent effort that goes into the task. Vanda could rise to the challenge of a task when she saw value in it. On the other hand, when she saw the task as merely time-filling, unrelated to any larger context, seemingly too difficult, or simply tedious, she would respond with a reduced effort and a reduced quality of result. Vanda and her colleagues with learning difficulties refuse to play the game of "school". And, because, from time to time, the rules of the game require that students perform activities which to them are without point or purpose, they produce inferior work.

Not that normal students never do this. They can be frequently inconsistent in their level of performance—but not to the same extent and not with the same results. For normal adolescents, a piece of inferior work is a signal to "pull up their socks", a signal that not enough effort went into the finished product. For adolescents with learning problems, a piece of inferior work usually reinforces their own negative perception of their ability, as well as the perception others have of them. The adolescent without learning problems is more willing to play the game of "school" or, at least, to accept the premise that some activities, while apparently without purpose in the immediate sense, may indeed be part of a long-range goal, the point of which will only become apparent over time.

At issue once more, is the crucial role of the teacher. It falls to the teacher to coax, cajole, propel, even manipulate the adolescent with learning problems into producing to potential and to clarify for that student both the means to complete an activity and the purpose for doing it. It is not enough to alter or even replace the curriculum when a student is not working to potential. What is needed is sound teaching strategy.

There is also a matter of trust. A student, who does not see purpose in an activity, will still perform that activity with intense and sincere effort, if he trusts the teacher. For students with learning difficulties, this becomes an even more fundamental concern. Because of their established history of failure, they will, in many cases, work to their potential only to please a teacher. Then, once a pattern of working to potential is established, the teacher has concrete examples with which to prove their own capacity for success. A momentum is established and the students will tend to work to potential for their own sake. The critical stage is generating that momentum, and that takes a teacher whom they will trust. No one knows better than teachers that this trust does not develop automatically.

Unwillingness To Defer Gratification

In the personal history of every adult who reads this book, there is at least one course from secondary school that brings back unpleasant memories. For me, it was algebra in the eleventh grade. Never was there a subject more abstruse and more utterly pointless—at least to me—than algebra.

My frustration with it had all the trappings. In class, the complexities of a quadrilateral equation would melt away under the teacher's inexorable logic. At home, alone, I couldn't get past square root. By contrast, I had classmates who could manipulate permutations and combinations as though they were born to the task. I, meanwhile, had foundered permanently on "solving for two unknowns". By mid-year I had developed a psychotic tic at the mention of "X".

Yet, because our high school had the good sense to average my algebra mark with history, French, and so on, I made it out of the eleventh grade and I never looked at algebra again.

The point of this bit of personal history is that it reveals a situation that was ripe for withdrawal, for "drop-out". Yet, that is not what happened. I needed algebra to complete the year and I knew that, relative to what my education could eventually do for me, algebra was worth the pain. Therefore, I stuck to it, and although maximum effort brought only minimal results, the ultimate balance was favourable. Most adolescents with learning difficulties would quite likely have withdrawn in those circumstances. They seem to have an unstated but dominating motto: "If at first you don't succeed—quit!"

To persist in the face of repeated failure certainly does not suggest superior intelligence; perhaps even the reverse is true. Yet, the fact remains that an adolescent who is learning normally is more likely to endure an unrewarding school situation or make adjustments to alleviate that situation than he is to withdraw—unlike his colleague with a learning problem. The difference seems to be in their respective objectives and long-term goals. The former student comprehends a difficult situation as only part of his total experience. There is also a capacity for hope and optimism, built up through years of success. The adolescent with learning problems, because of his probable history of failure, low self-esteem, and low expectations, does not see light at the end of the tunnel. He doesn't even look for it. All he sees is failure in the present. If he thinks of the future at all, it is likely in very bleak terms. No wonder then, that, without immediate gratification, without some immediate success, this student will simply quit. What is the point of deferring gratification when gratification will never come?

Here, again, the position of the teacher becomes a central one. The student's unwillingness to defer gratification is real and, until it is overcome, the likelihood of his completing any task is remote. What he needs is the confidence that comes with success. And he needs this success on a regular basis. Success does for a student with learning problems what sunshine does for a stained glass window. A teacher can arrange this. With long range goals in mind, but not stated, the teacher must structure the curriculum for this student so that he is aware of incremental gains. The size of these increments and the amount to be covered between each plateau of success depend upon the teacher's perception of the student's needs. Likewise, the content, the manipulation of sequence, the increase or reduction in challenge must all be controlled by the teacher. It is not a structural design that can be imposed by any other authority; to overcome the unwillingness to defer gratification requires the immediate hand of the classroom teacher.

Perceived Disassociation from the Mainstream

There were 32 students in 4G9F. An equal balance of boys and girls and the average age was 15.5. While they were not dramatically different from any of my other "special" classes, they seemed to have acquired that spirit of collective resistance to enthusiasm much earlier in the school year than was customary. That is, until we began the technique of brainstorming.

When the idea was first introduced, it was met with what I have come to call the Litany of the Problem Student!

"It's dumb!" "Yeah".
"It stinks!" "Yeah".
"We done that awready!" "Yeah".
"Wadda we gotta do this for?" "Yeah".

But for reasons I've never quite understood, brainstorming caused 4G9F to catch fire. We brainstormed imaginary problems; we brainstormed real problems. We used the technique in the curriculum; we even demonstrated it for other classes.

The crowning touch came about three weeks before a Parent's Night cum Open House held at our school. 4G9F came up with over 150 ideas for this problem:

You are about to embark on a six-hour train ride during which you will be in charge of your seven-year-old nephew and your eight-year-old niece. What are some of the things you might do to keep them occupied during the trip?[1]

---

[1]*Thinklab 2*, © 1976, Science Research Associates, Toronto.

The 150 ideas were edited, typed, and published in a little booklet that was distributed on Open House night. It was the hit of the evening and 4G9F's morale went right off the scale.

Two weeks later, the annual United Appeal campaign was to begin. Classes in the school competed in an effort to raise funds and I expected 4G9F to pitch in wholeheartedly, swept up in the wave of enthusiasm they had themselves created. They flatly refused.

"Let them *do it" was 4G9F's response.*

"If they want to raise money so badly, it's up to them."

"Them" for adolescents with learning problems is everyone else in a school. "They" are the successful students, the ones who appear to be coping splendidly, the students for whom the school seems to have been created. As well "they" are often the teachers, the administration, and anyone else who is deemed to have official capacity in making the school function.

Schools, offices, hospitals—any organizations which have about them a sense of self-sufficiency, a sense of intact and semi-isolated community within themselves—have as a result a kind of special atmosphere, an ethos which is impossible to identify specifically. A stranger in a school or hospital senses it immediately. He is not trespassing, yet he knows he is intruding. On the other hand, those who are part of the special community draw comfort and security from their involvement. For newcomers, there is always an awkward period before they are assimilated; for old-timers, there is a great reluctance to leave. Every one of these special communities has its own set of unwritten doctrines, guiding principles which shape behaviour and attitude. These are the rules by which the game is played in that community. Invariably, those who most enjoy their situation and who are most successful in it are the people who accept and practise the rules of the game.

Whether the game of "school" is a good or bad thing is not the point. What is important is that it is real and that so many adolescents with learning difficulties do not play it. Some reject it reflexively, as they reject everything. Others, whose resentment is less deeply rooted, just ignore it. Some simply do not know how to play. But what all of them have in common is a perception that the game was designed for others.

Given the tradition, especially in secondary schools, of championing academic success above all else, this perception may not be all that inexact. Schools typically represent the dominant culture and it follows that the game will be built on the dominant culture's rules. Since many adolescents with problems are not part of the dominant culture, it is hard for them to play. Even the architecture of secondary schools frequently militates against the "problem" students, isolating them in the "technical wing", the ESN block, or, as my students in one school called it, "the dummy ward".

There are penalties for not playing the game and these penalties cost the adolescent with learning difficulties. For one thing, he does not receive the emotional reward and, thereby, the momentum and security that come from being part of the community. As his sense of isolation from the mainstream increases, his sense of resistance and rejection develops with it. There are many adolescents, particularly the older ones, who would *rather* be outside the mainstream.

To alter this situation is difficult and delicate. Certainly, the way in which a school is administered can have a vital impact. Even its size and its design can have an effect. However, it is ultimately the teacher's task to demonstrate that the school does exist for the students with learning problems. Because the adolescent with learning problems forms opinions suspiciously and tentatively, his attitude to the game of "school" is very likely to be shaped by what he initially determines is the school's perception of him. And *that* he will learn from his classroom teachers.

Lack of Self Esteem

In my very first semester as a teacher, I was required to present a carefully laundered version of Greek mythology to A9C, a bright-eyed, bumptious group of academically inclined adolescents, and to Prep 9F, my first group of learning-problem adolescents. ("Prep" stood for preparatory; I never did find out what they were being prepared for!)

The core of the programme was based on an awesomely dull prose version of the siege of Troy. Midway through our study, I held a contest. Each class was divided into two teams and quizzed competitively on names, events, relationships, etc. When I suggested the teams pick names for themselves, A9C decided on the Trojan Warriors vs. the Grecian Lancers. 9F called themselves the Shitheads and the Dumbells!

Whenever teachers debate the characteristics of adolescents with learning difficulties, the single and most overwhelming feature on which the discussion inevitably comes to rest is lack of self-esteem. It is a widely-known and uncomfortable truth that these young people simply do not think very much of themselves. The consequences permeate just about every aspect of their school careers. Instead of approaching tasks with confidence, these students are tentative and easily discouraged. Lack of self-esteem dulls their sensitivity, lowers their capacity for fascination, and almost obliterates their curiosity. In sum, it produces the one thing that teachers find almost impossible to overcome: *indifference.* More good things in school are lost because of indifference than are lost because of active rejection. Dealing with indifference causes teachers much more pain than dealing with hostility. Yet, indifference is the first thing a teacher must try to sweep aside.

Impaired Cognitive Efficiency

The dialogue that follows is fictional, but conversations like this are a daily occurrence in the careers of teachers who work with adolescents who have learning difficulties.

> Teacher: *"Have you finished your assignment?"*
> Student: *"What assignment?"*
> Teacher: *"The one I gave you yesterday; the one that was supposed to be completed for today."*
> Student: *"Oh, that assignment. Yeah, I've got it."*
>
> *(from a hip pocket comes a slightly tattered, irregularly folded piece of notepaper)*
>
> Teacher: *"This is it?"*
> Student: *"Yep"*
> Teacher: *"Do you need these two telephone numbers? Or what about this exercise that looks like it came from Ms. K 's math class?"*
> Student: *"Yeah, we had math this morning and I didn't have my book so . . ."*
> Teacher: *"But you haven't finished your assignment. There were eight questions. There are only five here!"*
> Student: *"There is — I mean — there are? I mean — yeah, I guess I didn't."*
> Teacher: *"And where's the answer to question one? Your answers start at number two."*
> Student: *"That? Oh, that's in my science book."*
> Teacher: *"Your science book!"*
> Student: *"Yeah, I didn't have the right book in your class yesterday, so . . ."*
> Teacher: *"Well, where's your science book?"*
> Student: *"At home."*
> Teacher: *"At home! But you have science next period!"*
> Student: *Yeah, I thought it was Thursday."*
> Teacher: *"Can't you get it at lunch? You only live across the street."*
> Student: *"Naw. Y'see my mother, she's workin' and I'm supposed to have a key, but . . ."*

Any analysis of adolescents with learning difficulties will inevitably and logically deal first with the behavioural side of these students, for this is the most dramatic, the most obvious side. Yet, interwoven with all the behaviours that these students present is a subtle but profoundly important cognitive element. Put simply, these students just do not think efficiently. In fact, it may well be that much of the unproductive behaviour is a direct result of impaired cognitive efficiency. The preceding imaginary conversation is so familiar to teachers because it reflects the desperately ineffectual cognitive style manifested by so many adolescents with learning problems. For the student in this conversation, the operative phrase by which he explains himself to the world is: "*I forgot.*" Indeed, forgetting is convenient; it enables one to avoid all kinds of reality. But to regard this as solely an avoidance technique is not enough. The habit of forgetting is partly an outgrowth of his cognitive style, his failure to plan ahead, and his failure to think in terms of consequences and hypotheses. ("If I do this, then ..." or "If I fail to do this, then ...").

Lack of forward planning and lack of consequential thinking are not the only areas of cognitive deficiency that teachers see in these students. Concomitant with these features is a striking inability to organize, to follow a systematic process, to reason and deduce. Just to follow a procedure in sequence is sometimes an overwhelming task. The results, while sometimes funny, are also sad, as in the following situation. Unlike the previous dialogue, this one is true. As always, the names are changed.

> *The work experience programme at our school included training in telephone reception service. We had a special switchboard which enabled instructors to hear not only the student operator, but the voice of the incoming caller as well.*
>
> *When Rosa, aged 16, was given her first opportunity to be the school's telephone receptionist, she had, of course, been trained in the proper sequence:*
>
> 1. *Answer with a polite, cheerful "Good morning, Baxter Secondary School."*
> 2. *Determine who is being called.*
> 3. *Politely ascertain the name of the caller ("May I ask who's calling, please?")*
>
> *There was particular emphasis on the importance of Step Three since our school received many strange calls.*
>
> *Rosa's very first incoming call went exactly like this:*
>
> Rosa: *"Good morning! Baxter Secondary School."*
> Caller: *"Hello. May I speak to Miss Cherney?"*
> Rosa: *"What's your name?"*
> Caller: *"Kathy Brent."*
> Rosa: *"Who?"*
> Caller: *"Kathy Brent."*
> Rosa: *"There's nobody here named Kathy Brent!"*
>
> *And with righteous satisfaction, she cut the line.*

It is important to point out that Rosa was most emphatically not retarded. Nor did she fall into any of those categories that float around the periphery of that label, like "educable retarded" or "borderline retarded". Indeed, she was slower to grasp instructions and slower to follow them, but she had the potential to do so. What was "wrong" with Rosa, if "wrong" is the word to be used, was that her cognitive potential had never been tapped. Rosa followed a life style that generally did not require her to deal with more than one thing at a time. Her ability to process a sequence—to organize, to engage in forward planning, to reason and deduce—was rarely called upon. Thus, in a moment of intensity, her first incoming call, complete with listening instructors standing around her, Rosa simply did not perform.

At a variety of levels and in a variety of environments, the same thing that happened to Rosa happens to other adolescents who have been identified as having learning problems. Their school performance is reduced because of their inefficient cognitive styles.

This phenomenon is sometimes rationalized in terms of their cultural background—the fact that there may be a mismatch between the demands of a middle class curriculum structure and the cognitive style of students who grow up in an environment deprived of the features of the dominant culture. Other explanations suggest that members of subcultural groups are uncomfortable with the syntax and vocabulary of the dominant culture's language; since language is such an essential ingredient in the cognitive processes needed in school, these people are at a disadvantage. One of the most persistent beliefs is the one that describes adolescents with learning problems as being unable to think in abstract concepts. With the inevitable nod to Piaget, proponents of this explanation argue that these are students who have not yet grown from the concrete thinking stage to Piaget's "formal operations" or abstract thinking stage. Piaget says that this latter stage develops normally at about age eleven or twelve.

A more recent and considerably more intriguing explanation of cognitive inefficiency comes from the fields of neuro-anatomy and neuro-psychology. Since the middle of this century, it has been quite clearly established that the two hemispheres of the human brain are specialized for different kinds of cognitive processing: the left hemisphere for verbal, linear, logical, and precise processing and the right hemisphere for spatial, imaginative, appreciative, and more generalized activity. The right hemisphere perceives the whole and how it works; the left perceives the parts and catalogues the name of each in a specific sequence. It has been further established that, in most humans, one of the hemispheres tends to be dominant. That is, the style in which an individual thinks will usually be governed by one or other of the hemispheres. Either he will tend to be precise, logical, organized, and verbally adept or he will be rather generalized, not terribly concerned with organization or sequence, uncomfortable with words, but often imaginative and sensitive. What recent research[1] suggests is that successful students are those with a dominant left hemisphere. Since schools lean toward verbal, logical, and sequential processing, students who think that way meet the demands very well. The obvious corollary is that those who do not think in this style will find school more difficult.

Certainly, this theory is credible in terms of the cognitive styles that teachers see on a day-to-day basis among their students with learning problems. In fact, with the exception of the concrete versus abstract proposition, which most teachers find naive, each of the preceding explanations is indeed reflected in the reality of the classroom. In an immediate and practical sense, however, the neuro-psychological hypothesis is, by far, the most attractive.

It is attractive because it explains so clearly why Student A in auto shop will identify a faulty carburetor, smoothly dismantle and repair it, and reinstall it on the engine but, an hour later, will struggle agonizingly while trying to read a simple explanation of a carburetor's function. It explains why Student B will look at her teacher with complete innocence and say: "But I *know* how it goes together, why do I have to read the directions?" Or Student C who volunteers to restore order to a cupboard, does so with efficiency, and can, at any later time, put his finger on an item in the cupboard without hesitation, yet cannot describe to someone else how to find that same item. Or Student D who plays in a band and retains the arrangements for over 50 songs in her head, but is boggled by the 9 times table.

The theory is further attractive because it explains why students with such unfailing resources outside school (where the right hemisphere has more currency) defy the most prodigious teaching efforts between 9 a.m. and 3 p.m. But, most of all, it is attractive because it offers a teacher *something to do*. Just as research has demonstrated the problems, it has also shown that practice in appropriate thinking styles will enhance these students' abilities to perform in school. In other words, the problem of impaired cognitive efficiency is one that can be overcome by teaching.

Young people with learning difficulties can be helped to overcome those difficulties through cognitive training.[2] By tapping their cognitive potential, by teaching them efficient cognitive strategies, they can be taught to deal more effectively with the challenges they face inside and outside school. The argument makes sense, if only by empirical evidence

---

[1]For an excellent review of the literature, as well as an explanation of the brain in lay person's terms, see Wittrock, M.C. (ed.), *The Human Brain*. Englewood Cliffs, N.J.: Prentice-Hall, 1977.

[2]Chapter 8 is devoted to a practical programme on this issue.

alone. If these students, these six-hour mentally retarded individuals, can function successfully outside school, then it is obvious they have resources. The resources are simply not being used effectively between 9 a.m. and 3 p.m.

To teach thinking, then, to teach efficient cognitive strategies to students who are having obvious difficulties in school because of their failure to think effectively, seems eminently logical. Students, who are not succeeding because they fail to organize, because they do not think in terms of hypotheses and consequences, or because they do not process in sequence or explore systematically, could clearly benefit from being taught these strategies. Once again, the role of the classroom teacher is in the forefront. It's the teacher who must expose them to these strategies.

Sooner or Later: Avoidance

All human beings indulge in avoidance from time to time. Everyone has had a headache, real or imagined, when confronted with an unpleasant or difficult task. There are variations on the headache theme. Some people have stomach aches; others misplace their eyeglasses. Some become sleepy; others rush hither and yon in a burst of frenetic activity, completing a whole range of inconsequential tasks. Avoidance is a very common, very ordinary occurrence. What distinguishes the avoidance behaviour of an adolescent with learning problems is that, for him, it is almost a way of life. Avoidance is the rule, not the exception.

All the characteristics of this adolescent culminate at some point in avoidance. And the performance of avoidance is almost always dramatic and sometimes bizarre. To obscure any perception of themselves as failures, some will engage in deceptions that are both grandiose and pathetic. A colleague of mine once showed me a large cardboard box filled with a "novel". It was the effort of a student about to be transferred to our school. He had, laboriously and singlehandedly, copied out the entire text of Jules Verne's *Twenty Thousand Leagues Under the Sea* and presented it to her as a story he had written! Others engage in a form of self-delusion that is almost unshakable. One of our students, who was quite severely physically handicapped, dismissed the importance of improving her reading ability as totally unnecessary because she was going to become a physical education teacher. Some deliberately act out to avoid being confronted with challenges that they fear will reveal weaknesses. A typical case was Andy, a twelve year old, who was transferred to my class in mid-semester. Andy used learning materials in a way that forced his teachers to take them away from him. Pens and pencils were used to jab those seated near him. Hardcover books were noisemakers. With paperbacks, he riffled the pages over and over. Rulers were vibrated under his thigh. For peace and safety, teachers had to take materials from him and, naturally, then, he could not work. Still others blithely tune out, such as the boy in a behavioural class in which the noise and activity levels were exceedingly high. This adolescent simply allowed himself to sink out of sight so that when, two weeks before the end of semester, his notebook was examined, it was found to contain 572 drawings of pine trees and *nothing* else!

The result of intense avoidance tactics is that the student misses the point being made, or does not develop the skill being taught, or does not receive the developmental practice he needs. Thus, he must avoid the next challenge, so that, in turn, he misses yet another point. So the cycle continues until the student is genuinely lost. His negative perception of himself, and the unflattering view of him likely to be held by all those who must deal with him, are based, therefore, on real factors.

Interrupting this cycle requires all the resources, personal and external, that a teacher can muster. It is a very unusual student who will achieve a rescue on his own. To change the environment may help; to alter the curriculum may too. But, to perceive, analyse, and curb the cycle of destructive avoidance behaviour requires a classroom teacher.

Postscript

Before this book goes any further, it may be useful to take a look at teachers as a professional group.[1] Obviously, the premise of this book is that the role of the teacher is seminal if there is ever to be any progress in the education of adolescents with problems in learning. From any perspective—empirical, theoretical, practical—the premise is irrefutable. Yet, herein lies the nub of a difficult and sensitive issue. Although no one with at least a reasonable grasp of what takes place in the learning process would argue against the vital *role* of the teacher, it would be foolish to assume that the mere *presence* of a teacher is sufficient to solve all problems. Because the teacher is the key to the adolescent with learning problems, it is entirely conceivable that the key may turn the wrong way! Fortunately, the incidence of such an outcome is far less frequent than the positive, successful turnings. But no one denies that it can happen. In other words, just being a teacher is not enough; it is only the first step.

Like other professions, teaching has potential problems that are inherent in the very nature of the work. Because they are responsible for managing large groups of young people with less experience and maturity than themselves, teachers may tend to become directive. A few become imperious. Hand-in-glove with this issue is the dangerous potential for becoming all-knowing. Teachers are relied upon to organ-

[1]Probably, this section should have been in the preface to the book, but no one reads prefaces, except reviewers, editors, and those students who are shrewd enough to use it to discover an author's intent. Better it should be read now.

ize, impart, process, and provide knowledge and information. It is easy to fall into the tension-filled trap of feeling obliged to have all the answers. There is also the frustration that builds when students not only fail to respond to the most massive teaching efforts, but even seem to resist those efforts. Added to these professional concerns are the niggling non-professional chores a teacher must do: taking attendance, collecting money, organizing health and community efforts, because school is a convenient place to accomplish this.

No one pretends that the task of teaching is easy—except for the layman who only counts teachers' vacation days. It is hard work and it is vital work. And, like any other profession in which its members have the key role in a process, the quality of the role depends upon the individual. What follows in this book are suggestions based on common sense and long experience with students who have learning difficulties. They are suggestions that, hopefully, will make the key role of the classroom teacher a little easier.

Bibliography

These reference works enhance the assumptions on which Chapter Three is based.

Blakeslee, T.R., *The Right Brain*. New York: Anchor Press, 1980.

Botkin, A., L. Schmaltz, and D. Lamb, 1977, "Overloading the Left Hemisphere in Right-handed Subjects with Verbal and Motor Tasks", *Neuropsychologia*, 15: 591-96.

Chall, J.S., and A.F. Mirsky, *Education and the Brain*, Seventy-seventh Yearbook of the National Society for the Study of Education. Chicago: University of Chicago Press, 1978.

Entwhistle, D.R., "Developmental sociolinguistics: Inner-city children", *American Journal of Sociology*, 1968, 74, 37-49.

Feuerstein, R., *The Dynamic Assessment of Retarded Performers*. Baltimore: University Park Press, 1979.

Feuerstein, R., *Instrumental Enrichment*. Baltimore: University Park Press, 1980.

Galin, D., and R. Ellis, 1975, "Asymmetry in Evoked Potentials as an Index of Lateralized Cognitive Processes: Relation to EEG Alpha Asymmetry", *Neuropsychologia*, 13: 45-50.

Goldberg, M.L., "Factors affecting educational attainment in depressed urban areas", in A.H. Passow (Ed.), *Education in depressed areas*. New York: Teachers College Press, 1963.

Goldberg, M.L., "Methods and materials for educationally disadvantaged youth", in A.H. Passow, M. Goldberg, and A.J. Tannenbaum (Eds.), *Education of the disadvantaged*. New York: Holt, Rinehart and Winston, 1967.

Haywood, H.C., "Cognitive Education for Learning Disabled Adolescents", *Journal of Abnormal Child Psychology*, 1980, 8(1), 51-64.

Hecaen, J., and J. Sauguet, 1971, "Cerebral Dominance in Left-handed Subjects", *Cortex*, 7: 19-48.

Hunt, J.M., "Environment, development, and scholastic achievement", in M. Deutsch, I. Katz, and A. Jensen (Eds.), *Social class, race, and psychological development*. New York: Holt, Rinehart, and Winston, 1968.

Kagan, J., "On cultural deprivation", in D.C. Glass (Ed.), *Environmental influences*. New York: Russell Sage Foundation, 1968.

Kershner, John R., 1975, "Reading and Laterality Revisited", *Journal Special Education*, 9(3): 269-79.

Kinsbourne, M., 1974, "Cerebral Control and Mental Evolution", in M. Kinsbourne and A. Smith (Eds.), *Hemispheric Disconnection and Cerebral Function*. Springfield, Ill.: Charles C. Thomas.

Knights, R.M., and D.J. Bakker, *The Neuropsychology of Learning Disorders*. Baltimore: University Park Press, 1976.

President's Committee On Mental Retardation, *The Six hour retarded child*. Washington, D.C.: U.S. Government Printing Office, 1970.

Sherman, J., R. Kulhavy, and K. Burns, 1976, "Cerebral Laterality and Verbal Processes", *J. Exper. Psych.*, 2(6): 720-27.

Segalowicz, S.J., and F.H. Gruber, *Neurological Theory and Language*. New York: Academic Press, 1977.

Sigel, I.E., "Some thoughts on directions for research in cognitive development", in *Perspectives on Human deprivation: Biological, psychological and sociological*. Washington, D.C.: U.S. Department of Health, Education and Welfare, 1968.

Sperry, R.W., 1967, "Split-Brain Approach to Learning Problems", G.C. Quarton, R. Melnechuk, and E.C. Schmitt (Eds.), *The Neurosciences: A study Program*. New York: Rockefeller Univ. Press.

Waksman, M., *Assessment of the Effects of Instrumental Enrichment, Cognitive Training On the Intellectual Performances of Basic Level Students at A Vocational High School*, Commissioned Study By the Ontario Ministry of Education, 1979.

Waksman, M., H. Silverman, and K.J. Weber, "Assessing The Learning Potential of Penitentiary Inmates", 1981, (in press).

Weber, K.J., "On Making Reading Tests Useful For Teachers", *Proceedings of York University Conference on Reading*, 1980.

Wiig, E.H., and E.M. Semel, *Language disabilities in children and adolescents*. Columbus, Ohio: Charles E. Merrill, 1976.

Witelson, Sandra F., 1977, "Developmental Dyslexia: Two Right Hemispheres and None Left", *Science*, 195: 309-11.

CHAPTER 4
SETSEM: A TEACHING MODEL

EASILY THE most memorable student and all-star character I have ever taught or, rather, tried to teach, was a young man of 15 named Sully. He was brought to our probation-resource[1] *class one morning in early November and turned over with the admonition: "You like these students; see what you can do with this one!"*

With Sully came a very thick file of reports, assessments, and learned opinions. Since I deliberately ignore these for at least two weeks to avoid being prejudiced by other opinions, I was unaware that Sully had one of the sharpest wits I would ever encounter in my career. Not only the wit but the tongue to match. Sully honed both on his slower classmates and turned them loose on his teachers. To complete the profile, Sully was a repository of all the great lines and quips ever uttered. His heroes were people like Robert Benchley, Dorothy Parker, Mark Twain, and he seemed to be able to adapt and use everything they'd ever said. Sully used this talent to accomplish something on my behalf: he convinced a student teacher to reconsider her choice of career.

This young person was clearly one of those people who should not have chosen teaching. She was without patience, had remarkably little insight into human nature for one so intelligent, and simply did not like students—especially Sully's class. To compound matters, she had an odd quirk of classroom management whereby any departure from the behavioural norm would elicit a frown, a sneer, a grimace—some facial expression indicating extreme distaste. As Sully later described her (via P.G. Wodehouse), "She could open an oyster at fifty feet with her left eye!"

The crunch came when she passed a set of dictionaries among the boys, then proceeded to write single words on the

[1]A unique group who, with their supposed learning problems, shared a history of conflict with the law.

chalkboard. The boys were to read the dictionary definition in chorus. It was an incredibly dull operation and Sully watched the process in mild disbelief for the first few words. Then she wrote ENVIOUS in big block letters on the chalkboard. Sully yawned, long and loud. It was a challenge.

"You! You there! Are you asleep?!"

"Me? Me? Oh no, ma'am, I'm . . . I'm . . . I'm envious. I'm envious."

"Oh really now! Envious of what?"

"Of my foot, ma'am. It's asleep!"

It was all downhill from that point. The next day, she refused to teach Sully's class and, within a week, had withdrawn from her teacher education course. I have never seen her since, but I suspect she is probably successful in whatever other career she chose. She was a very intelligent and able person but not suited for teaching.

She was also a victim of circumstance. Her own experience as a student was in the tradition of "The teacher is always right. Obey." Even if adolescents with learning problems were acquainted with that tradition, it is highly unlikely they would acknowledge it, let alone accept it. To deal with this type of student, simply to be *the teacher* is not enough. For these young people, there must be a very carefully thought-out teaching plan.

The SETSEM Teaching Model

Before any productive teaching plan can be developed for adolescents with learning difficulties, there are certain factors that must be taken into account. To begin with, these students practise compensatory avoidance behaviours which make the act and art of teaching them difficult. Interwoven with this reality is the fact of their adolescence. These students are experienced. They are familiar with the strategies on *both* sides of the teacher's desk. When they respond to a new approach with "We done that awready", it is usually because they already have! Not only have they "done it awready" but, in their perception, the approach was ineffective then and will be ineffective now. Adolescents in this group have lost much of their capacity for faith and for hope.

Who can blame them? There are few adolescents with learning difficulties whose problems become illuminated only at the time of adolescence. Now, with the reality of *post*-school life near, they find themselves *still* in the learning difficulty camp. No wonder they are cynical. No wonder they reject curriculum that is obviously a diluted version of the "normal". And no wonder they are unwilling to welcome another reworking of teaching strategies that have been unsuccessful.

In spite of this, the development of a productive teaching plan for these young people does not have to be based on anything radical or dramatic. What is necessary is the simple recognition of their needs as adolescents: their need for success, for security, and for hope; their need for training in efficient ways of thinking which will have an impact on their academic performance and on their life-competence; their need for intrinsic, not imposed, momentum; and their need for clear direction, a perception that there is light at the end of the tunnel. Above all, they must be cognizant that everything being done for them in school is part of a consistent, clearly organized plan for reaching that light.

The SETSEM Teaching Model is a modest proposal for meeting these needs. It is based on experience, practicality, common sense, research, and a recognition that the teacher is the key. Subsequent chapters elaborate on each of the important elements in the model. At this point, it should suffice simply to explain what these elements are.

The SETSEM Model

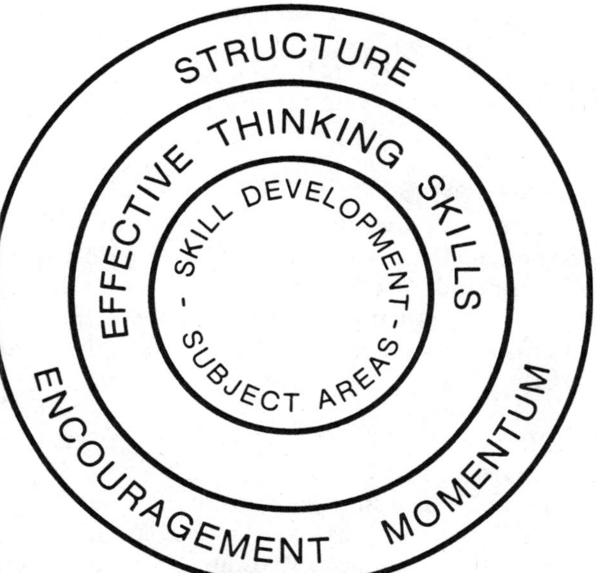

S structure,

E efficient —

T thinking skills.

S skill development/subject areas.

E encouragement.

M momentum.

Structure

A common difficulty faced by adolescents with learning problems is the apparent disorganization in their school and personal lives. Most of them have a history of indecision, of failed and incomplete attempts, and of uncertain direction. By adolescence, their vague distrust of school has usually been confirmed. They have little faith that anything concrete or productive will ever be done for them. The so-called "normal" student, by adolescence, has usually developed an overview of what is happening in the educational process, or, at least, is aware of a pattern in which he perceives that each of the parts is designed to form a whole. At least, he usually *trusts* that this is so. His colleague with learning problems does not enjoy the benefits of this perception. For him, the parts are unconnected fragments; there is no whole. It is necessary, therefore, to devise a programme that has clear direction, that establishes reasonable but specific expectations and behaviour, and that establishes incremental plateaus of opportunity and success. Without a structure in which the goals, the activities, the parameters, and the appropriate behaviours are specific and clear to the students, no teaching plan can be effective for them. Certainly, such structure must obtain in the classroom. Ideally, it will be present in the entire school environment as well.[1]

Efficient Thinking Skills

Since one of the major reasons for the difficulties these adolescents face in school is their inefficient and undeveloped cognitive abilities, it is reasonable to conclude that learning efficient strategies of thinking should be a vital part of their programme. However, like all self-evident truths, this is easier to talk about than bring about. (It also accounts for the fact that the chapter on teaching efficient thinking skills is the largest one in this book).

In the SETSEM model, students learn these strategies through practice with material that is not curricular-specific. Very simply, the process involves teaching a strategic concept such as *systematic exploratory behaviour* with material that is not related specifically to any traditional subject in the academic curriculum. Once the concept is understood, and students use it automatically, *then* they are encouraged to

---

[1]Mandatory reading for every administrator and teacher involved with the adolescent is the research published by Michael Rutter and his colleagues in *Fifteen Thousand Hours* (Cambridge: Harvard University Press, 1979). In this project, Rutter *et al* present overwhelmingly convincing evidence of the profound effect that the structure of an individual school can have on students' achievements, behaviour, and attitudes. The report by James S. Coleman, "Public and Private Schools", released in 1981, shows that schools in the United States reflected exactly the same effect: overall school policies and structures do indeed have a powerful impact on students' achievement and behaviour.

apply it to the regular curriculum. In effect, it is a procedure principally devoted to teaching the logical, analytical strategies of the left hemisphere to young people who do not usually think this way. Certainly, one might argue that the regular curriculum can form the immediate base for teaching efficient thinking strategies and that the use of non-curricular specific material is superfluous. Such an argument fails to take into account one of the salient features of the adolescent with learning difficulties. The regular curriculum represents that which students have already failed. Not that the regular curriculum should be set aside. Rather, the temporary use of material that is non-curricular specific, something which they have not yet failed, is designed to give the students strategies which will improve their competence with the regular curriculum. In short, the SETSEM model suggests that one teaches efficient cognitive strategies *prior* to and, subsequently as part of, the regular curriculum.

Subject Areas

Traditional subjects must be included in a teaching plan for adolescents with learning difficulties. These adolescents already feel a sense of isolation. To deny them the subjects which they know the "normal" students take will compound that isolation and generate resentment.

The SETSEM model does not presume to suggest how the content of specific subjects should be taught. However, it does suggest that these traditional subjects should be taught in a specifically structured context, and that students should be prepared for dealing with these subjects by prior and concomitant training in the cognitive skills necessary to handle them.

Further, with the possible exception of certain technical skill areas, it is important that teachers of traditional subjects avoid regarding their subjects as ends in themselves. Given the nature of the university training most teachers of adolescents have received, this is sometimes a difficult task. At a university, the various subject disciplines tend to be approached as very specific entities with little attention paid to the place of that entity in the context of other subject entities. The result is that, all too frequently, a teacher of adolescents learns to regard himself as a teacher of "English", or "Mathematics", or "Science", rather than as a teacher of students *first* and, *then*, a teacher of English, Mathematics, or Science.

The tendency is natural. Because a teacher of adolescents has usually "specialized" at a university, he graduates having spent a great deal of time in a highly specific atmosphere and at a level of advanced competence. It is only natural that a teacher would want to impart some of his specialized knowledge to willing, eager, and, as yet, unformed minds, to stimulate the same respect for his subject that he developed in his university studies. Usually, the first ten minutes of a career with adolescents who have learning difficulties is sufficient to set that illusion straight. Yet, there is potential for great danger here.

Once a teacher of adolescents discovers that only a strikingly small minority of them are as interested in his subject as he is, he must struggle to avoid two very inviting traps. One is to withdraw from the majority who do not appreciate the subject. The other is to react with remedial fanaticism and to spend a great deal of time in the basic groundwork of a subject to make students *able* to comprehend and appreciate its glories. The students are often finished school before those glories are ever reached.

The various subject areas in a curriculum are vital to a productive teaching plan for adolescents with learning difficulties. What teachers must seek to do is to extract from their respective subjects the maximum benefit for the ultimate careers of these students. Subjects are not ends; they are means for developing the life-competence, the humanity, and the sensitivity of those who study them.

Skill Development

One of the facts of life in teaching adolescents with learning problems is that they frequently seem to be deficient in basic skills such as reading, spelling, and arithmetic. Much of a teacher's energy must go to meeting this reality. The skill development component in the SETSEM model does not deny this fact, although there are three major points to consider.

In the first place, adolescents with learning difficulties usually appear to be much more deficient than they really are. With the exception of some of the very seriously handicapped, these adolescents inevitably have a higher level of basic competence than they customarily demonstrate and, certainly, a higher level than will be revealed by a rigidly timed, norm-referenced, standardized achievement test. By simply being in school for all this time, these students have acquired a range of skills. There is also the factor of what is often called "street smarts" or "street sharps". These six-hour mentally retarded adolescents are competent outside school and utilize a range of basic skills in that environment. The problem is that this battery of skills, acquired both in school and out, is disorganized, erratic, and incomplete. Herein lies the second major point.

A programme in skill development must include cognitive training to help these adolescents organize, inter-relate, and use the skills they already have, *and* incorporate the new ones being learned.

The third point has to do with classroom organization and structure. The teaching of basic skills should take place in individualized programmes. If one were to isolate a basic skill, select any group of adolescents with learning problems, and plot on a graph their individual ability profiles in that skill, the plot-line would unquestionably be irregular and saw-toothed. There are few homogeneous ability groups among this type of adolescent. Thus, to teach a basic skill to an entire class of them simultaneously inevitably means that certain students will be under-challenged while others will be over-challenged. Both will react negatively, with all the attendant consequences. In the SETSEM model, skill development is an individualized procedure with each student being challenged by his own needs.

Encouragement

It is impossible to find the word that best captures all the facets of the affective domain, from both the teacher's and the student's point of view. Yet, that domain is crucial to any sense of progress or any sense of momentum in the education of adolescents with learning problems. Feelings cannot be separated from the act of learning, in humans at least.

One might argue that the word *encouragement* is used here principally because it provides the vowel needed to complete the construction of an acronym: SETSEM. Indeed, it may fulfill that purpose, but the choice of the word was not made with quite so shallow an intent. The SETSEM model is a *teaching* model, not a technical, lock-step procedure. And it is based on what *can be* in every classroom, not on what might be, if only certain conditions would obtain. Therefore, it is essential that so vital a human component in the teaching-learning process—encouragement—be included, if only to acknowledge what all good teachers do as a matter of course. It is encouragement and all the other affective processes of which it is a part that elevate teaching and learning above mere mechanics. Encouragement infuses the way a teacher plans for his students, the way he organizes and presents a learning experience for them, even the way he evaluates them. It is often the only tool a teacher has available when dealing with an adolescent in full retreat from learning. Moreover, encouragement is symbolic. It demonstrates the teacher's acknowledgement that, no matter what the apparent level of function may be among his students, they are capable of more, of better. It is an affirmation of belief in their potential.

No teaching model can be effective over the long term without recognition of the affective domain. Yet, encouragement is reflective of a reality in the teaching-learning process in a way that other words may not be—namely, that, even though a teacher may open the road and pave the way, it is still the student's responsibility to travel it. This is where the final component of the SETSEM model comes in: *momentum*.

Momentum

The word and the concept are important. Momentum in the SETSEM model is not a mistaken substitute for motivation. Motivation is too often seen only as an extrinsic phenomenon by teachers. For some strange reason, it is a factor in the learning process for which teachers often feel solely responsible, and that it must be generated, therefore, by the dynamics of their teaching styles and the force of their personalities. Some teachers, by virtue of their innate talents, are very successful in motivating reluctant students. Usually, their talent is not a learned one but a natural one. Most teachers, in fact, most human beings, have this talent to a greater or lesser degree. The problem arises when large groups, that are generally resistant, need to be motivated on a daily basis. Even those teachers with the greatest gifts run out of energy eventually.

Other teachers, with less certainty of their capacity for stimulating adolescents, will look to specific teaching materials as the chief motivator. Publishers and programme designers continually flood the educational market with "high interest" items, their chief value being, presumably, their ability to motivate. Unfortunately, even these materials pall over time and teachers are forced to look for new materials before the inevitable "We done that awready" takes over.

Still other teachers—fortunately, these are few—rely on externally imposed rules and requirements to regulate the classroom process. There is no real concern for motivation because "This is what the school (substitute where applicable: the course of study, the board, the LEA, the Department) says you have to do, so . . ." or students might also hear: "If you want to get a certificate, then you have to . . .". To adolescents, who perceive themselves as dissociated from the mainstream, who care little for the authority of the "school", such an explanation is meaningless. Little wonder that teachers using this approach are the least likely to welcome a group of adolescents with learning problems into their timetables.

The problem lies simply in the concept of motivation. As long as the responsibility for motivation is presumed to be the teacher's, there will continue to be a relentless draining of resources both personal and material. As long as motivation is perceived by students with learning difficulties to be an extrinsic phenomenon in their education, they will passively permit everyone else to provide stimulation. In fact, by adolescence, this attitude tends to be a common one.

To shift the principle from one of motivation to one of momentum requires a shift in the teacher's viewpoint. Momentum is an *intrinsic* phenomenon and it is one that, once begun, generates its own force. Once a student with learning difficulties has attained some momentum in his learning, he will begin to move forward on his own. He will become his own force. What the teacher must conceive as his responsibility, then, is to arrange the learning experience for his students so that the force will become operative, so that they will see success and achievement and, thereby, develop hope and faith—all essential elements in generating and maintaining momentum.

This can be achieved first by structuring long range goals into shorter increments. These must be plateaus that are not only attainable with relative immediacy but that are also *perceived to be attainable* in the shorter term. Secondly, it can be achieved by training in efficient thinking. Once students realize they have the potential for developing sound thinking strategies and can think their way through most problems, they also realize that they have the capacity for achievement. This realization, in turn, generates momentum.

Claudia, aged thirteen, provides a good example. She was assigned to my "resource" class for two days a week, the goal being to improve her language skills. Here is a sample of her writing ability from early September. (The name of the school is removed to preserve her anonymity.)

When I leave __________ I will
I would like to make hospial
and take temperlures and help people
when they are sad in the hospial
Changed hospial beds. When I leave
__________ would not want to be
a tailor. But I would like to be
a gardener. plant flowers fruit
trees, tuplips I won't plant tom
atoes because I hate them I would
like to be cashier like my
mother I would buy greater big
house I would let orphanng
~~L~~ children live in my house
and some of my friends.

Although one might identify a variety of needs in the preceding passage, it was decided that the two immediate goals for Claudia would be: (a) practice in identifying and in writing grammatically complete sentences in sequence and (b) developing the strategy of processing information in logical sequence. While considerable time and effort was devoted to these two objectives, it was also decided that Claudia should continue to write passages of prose on a twice-weekly basis no matter what their quality, since her regular teacher had already established the momentum of writing with reasonable ease. Here, after intense practice in a very structured and individualized programme, is an example of Claudia's writing at the beginning of April. Aside from an obvious improvement in her penmanship which, I suggest, is partly the result of greater effort through momentum and, aside from some unintended humour, typical of Claudia, there are some important points to note.

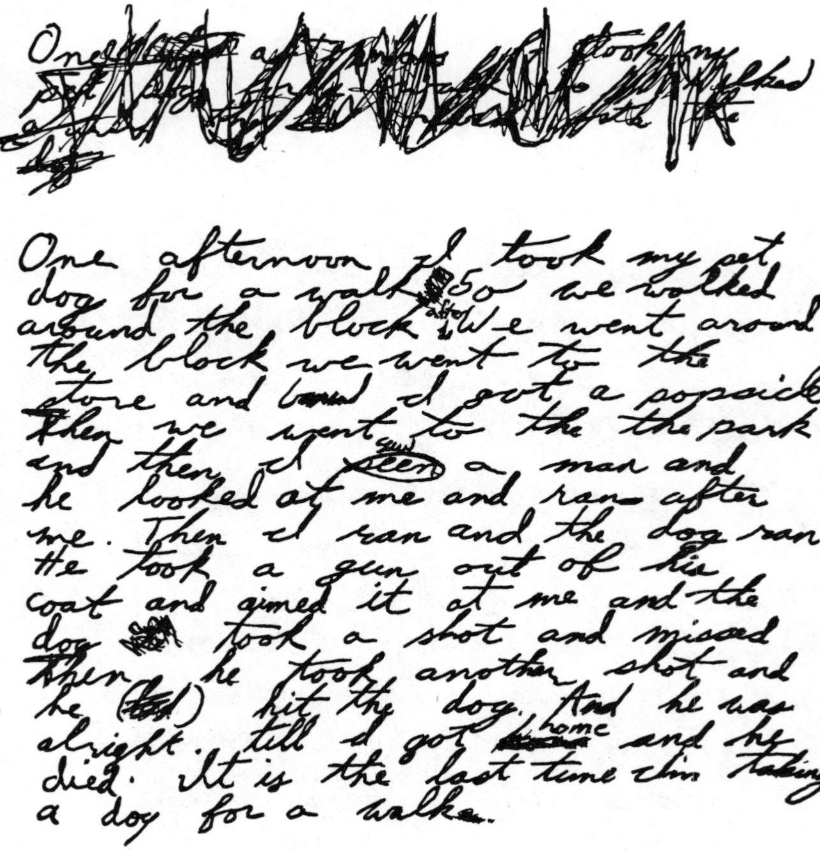
One afternoon I took my pet
dog for a walk so we walked
around the block after We went around
the block we went to the
store and I got a popsicle.
Then we went to the the park
and then I seen saw a man and
he looked at me and ran after
me. Then I ran and the dog ran.
He took a gun out of his
coat and aimed it at me and the
dog took a shot and missed
then he took another shot and
he hit the dog. And he was
alright till I got home and he
died. It is the last time I'm taking
a dog for a walk.

It is noteworthy that Claudia rejects her own first attempt and starts over. The willingness to begin again is a product of momentum. Secondly, there is obvious sequence. Each element in the story is processed in a logical order. Finally, and most interesting of all to her teachers, is the fact that she made four changes in the passage, on her own, to correct what would have been lapses in standard written English. Three of the four self-corrections were in sentence structure. Because the goals of her programme were clear to her, because she perceived them as attainable in a relatively immediate sense, and because she was helped to develop her potential for logical, sequential processing, Claudia had established her own momentum. All students have this capacity for momentum, the impetus and involvement that comes through clear direction and the satisfaction of accomplishment. It remains only for their teachers to arrange the possibility for them.

Momentum is a pivotal feature of the SETSEM model and, like each of the other elements in the model, it is part of an overall strategy designed to accommodate the needs of adolescents with learning problems. As a teaching plan, the SETSEM model is neither radical nor dramatic. And it most emphatically does not promise miracles. It does lay claim, however, to following the principles of reason and common sense, and certainly its components lie comfortably within the competence of anyone who chooses to try it. It does not require involved training or professional development, nor does it call for the purchase of expensive materials. All it needs is a teacher.

PART B

TEACHING THE ADOLESCENT WITH LEARNING DIFFICULTIES

CHAPTER 5
STRUCTURING SKILL DEVELOPMENT PROGRAMMES

SOONER OR LATER in that crucial first year, every novice teacher has the good sense or good fortune to find an ally on staff whose experience and wisdom is not merely beneficial but a life-saver. My saviour was a fine, old, and gentle man who taught metal-working. He had the gift of being paternal without being condescending, and not only the freshman teachers, but also his students, loved him for it.

The first time he saved me was from the trap in which so many first year teachers founder. There had developed, between my Prep Grade 9's and me, a tacit understanding that English class was to be entertaining, and that I was to be in charge of the entertainment. Having newly graduated with a flood of resources from my teacher training, and with the energy that comes with youth and novelty, I was remarkably successful until mid-semester, when I noticed that my resources and my energy were depleting rapidly and simultaneously. Much worse, there had developed a profound sense of ennui. There was an awareness, on both our parts, that nothing was being gained; there was no sense of accomplishment. We were all becoming restive, anxious, and mutually suspicious. When I confided this anxiety to my mentor, he quietly invited me to observe this same class in his metal-working shop.

During my visit there occurred one of those events that, to anyone but those involved, was quite insignificant. Yet, in retrospect, I'm certain it saved my career. One of my "trials" in the class was Angelo, a 15 year old with a long history of behavioural and academic problems; he was working diligently at a metal lathe. Apparently, I was unable to conceal my awe at his intense concentration. "Do you know what I like about this class?", he asked, without looking up. (Charitably, he did not add "as opposed to yours", although that was the clear implication.) "At least when you walk out of here, you can see what you've done."

It was that simple. In metal-working class, there was remarkably little of the entertainment that the Prep 9's had come to expect in my class. But there was order and structure, clear expectations, and, above all, a visible sense of accomplishment. Not only did the students in metal-working have a tangible record of their efforts, but they were also required to record their progress in a daily log—further concrete evidence of accomplishment. The progress recorded in the log was to dovetail, ideally, with a schedule of completed stages. This schedule had been drawn up under the teacher's guidance and in terms of each student's level of expertise. Students would assess their progress by comparing the schedule and their actual accomplishments as recorded. Prep 9 responded to this structure with enthusiasm and with a level of self-imposed obedience that was surprisingly rigorous.

The screwdriver that Angelo was making was hardly an exemplary model; yet, as he showed me later, it was a significant improvement over his earlier products. With each new screwdriver, his teacher had given him one or two new techniques to practise and develop. Instead of mounting a wide-ranging attack on all of Angelo's technical dificiencies in metal-working, the teacher had designed a programme to give Angelo specific areas in which to improve—tunnels with light at the end. Above all, Angelo was fully aware of the programme's design and of his progress in it. He had a clear perception of what was being done, of where he was going, and of his improvement. He had developed his own momentum. To Angelo, it was clearly a superior system to mine. To me, it was good fortune that I learned it in my first year. If it is successful in a technical subject, I reasoned, it can be successful with modification in an academic subject. And it is. However, like all useful, simple, and workable procedures, it is easier to operate than to describe. The several pages that follow imply much greater complexity than is really the case. In fact, to establish and operate individualized programmes in skill development is not complicated at all.

Establishing An Individualized Programme

Certain principles should obtain, no matter what variations one may wish to establish in the day-to-day operation of such a programme. In the first place, the programme for each student must indeed be individual.

Skills in which adolescents with learning problems are usually deficient, such as writing skills—punctuation, spelling, syntax, sentence structure—or arithmetic skills—addition, subtraction, multiplication, division—are skills which usually require considerable practice before mastery is achieved. Especially with this type of adolescent, mastery is achieved with great variations in amount of time and practice from individual to individual. It makes sense, therefore, to structure the system for independent practice, so that one student's speed or slowness does not become a personal disadvantage, because he is forced to follow an arbitrary pace and pattern established for a larger group. An independent programme, geared to the particular student's pace and using materials specifically selected for him, will neither frighten him into avoidance by excessive challenge nor bore him into mischief because the materials are inappropriate. The programme must also be *perceived* by the student to be an individual one. There can be little hope that momentum will develop unless this is the case.

A second principle is that it is essential for each student to adhere to some form of contract, schedule, or list on which specific objectives are detailed. These should be limited and attainable within the foreseeable future. This is not the place for listing long-range goals, even though these may be the teacher's ultimate purpose.

The third necessary element is a record of progress. This may take the form of a log, a chart, or any system by which the student can record and, therefore, *see* his increments of accomplishment on a day-to-day basis. Without a visible record of accomplishment, there is limited hope that a student will overcome the barrier of low self-esteem and there is every likelihood that he will continue to manifest a level of achievement that is well below his potential. A tangible record of accomplishment generates momentum.

The materials that are used in an individualized skill programme should ideally be those practice materials which a student can complete independently or, at least, with minimal direction. This is not to suggest that the teacher abdicates the role of instructor. On the contrary, much instruction will continue to take place. However, because it is likely to be on a one-to-one basis, instruction is also likely to be more efficient and, therefore, briefer, allowing more opportunity for the students to practise the skills being taught. For students with skill problems, particularly adolescents, it is often the lack of time and opportunity to practise a skill that accounts for their failure to acquire it.

A fifth principle is that time or, more specifically, timing, must be downgraded in importance. For adolescents with learning difficulties, time limits are the sword of Damocles. These students dismiss, reject, or avoid an activity because experience has taught them they will need more time to complete it than they will probably be allowed. An individualized programme must, by its very nature, adjust to the amount of practice a student will need and to the pace at which he works. His pace is likely to be a fairly well established character trait by adolescence.

Finally, in those situations where students meet a teacher on a regularly scheduled and reasonably frequent basis (i.e. as an English class, a science class, or a mathematics class), an individualized programme should take up only part of the time together. There must also be time for whole-class activities, for teacher-directed lessons which contribute not only to general learning but also to the feeling of belonging to a class or a group, an attachment which is vital to the morale of all adolescents.

Where students are withdrawn from an established group for special instruction on a periodic basis, it is conceivable that the individualized programme may come to operate full-time, especially since the purpose of such a withdrawal is to upgrade their skills so that they may return to the established group. Even in these situations, however, it may be productive to break out of the individualized pattern as frequently as the teacher's judgement deems it useful. Development of specific skills is important, but education has a wider base.

Overview of An Individualized Programme

Although the structure will vary according to individual teachers' preferences, the stages of this programme should follow this pattern.

Step One: Teacher informally identifies a range of needs evident in the skill profile of a student.

Step Two: Teacher selects a limited number of these for practice in the time set aside for individual skill development.

Step Three: Teacher puts together a package of materials which will provide opportunity for independent practice of the skills to be mastered.

Step Four: Teacher meets with student, having first listed on a contract the skills to be practised, and briefly explains what is necessary. Both sign the contract.

Step Five: Student works on materials in the learning package, as specified in the contract. Teacher provides one-to-one instruction, when necessary, and verifies that work is completed satisfactorily.

Step Six: At the end of each skill practice time, student records accomplishments on log or progress chart.

Step Seven: When the learning package has been completed, teacher assesses progress. A new contract, learning package, and progress chart are presented. Cycle begins again.

Operating An Individualized Programme

In several hundred workshops and seminars with teachers over the past several years, it has proven useful to outline the details of this programme by using an individual student's work as a point of reference. Here, then, is some work from Stanford, aged fourteen, who was a member of my resource room class, each of whose members were withdrawn from a regular class for special programmes in language arts and mathematics. This is an example of Stanford's writing when he first joined the class.

He Who Walks In Another's
Tracks Leaves No Footprints

I thik this sayig could have two menings. At lest It meens fist that you can wok in som others guys step like in the snow ~~and~~ if you put your foot on his ~~thw~~ you dont leve a mark theres more mening in this thow than is on the surfis I think the guy mens by this quotation that you dont have a chance of being anybody you cant be the leder all the time but you cant be following all the time otherwise your nothing

Here is an example of Stanford's work on a brief test with fractions, just before he was assigned to the class.

Compute and reduce to the lowest proper fraction.

$$\frac{4}{5} \times \frac{3}{7} = \frac{12}{35} \qquad \frac{7}{8} - \frac{2}{3} = \frac{21}{24} - \frac{16}{24} = \frac{5}{24}$$

$$\frac{9}{11} - \frac{2}{22} = \frac{7}{11} \qquad \frac{12}{13} \times \frac{1}{3} = \frac{12}{13} \times \frac{3}{1} = \frac{36}{13} = 2\frac{9}{13}$$

$$\frac{5}{8} \div \frac{1}{4} = \frac{5}{8} \times \frac{4}{1} = \frac{20}{8}$$

$$\frac{2}{5} \div \frac{2}{6} = \frac{2}{5} \times \frac{6}{2} = \frac{12}{10} = \frac{6}{5} = 1\frac{1}{5}$$

$$\frac{9}{13} \times \frac{1}{2} = \frac{9}{13} \times \frac{2}{1} = \frac{18}{13} = 1\frac{5}{13}$$

$$\frac{7}{12} \div \frac{2}{6} = \frac{14}{72} = \frac{7}{36}$$

$$\frac{8}{14} + \frac{3}{7} = \frac{8}{14} + \frac{6}{14} = \frac{14}{14}$$

$$4\frac{1}{2} \div 1\frac{1}{2} = \frac{9}{2} \times \frac{3}{2} = \frac{27}{4}$$

$$2\frac{3}{5} \times \frac{4}{5} = \frac{13}{5} \times \frac{5}{4} = \frac{13}{4}$$

$$7\frac{1}{3} \div 1\frac{1}{3} = \frac{22}{3} \times \frac{3}{4} = \frac{33}{6}$$

$$3\frac{4}{5} + 2\frac{1}{10} = \frac{38}{10} + \frac{21}{10} = \frac{59}{20}$$

$$1\frac{1}{2} - \frac{11}{12} = \frac{3}{2} - \frac{11}{12} = \frac{18}{12} - \frac{11}{12} = \frac{7}{12}$$

Determining Skills To Be Mastered (Step One)

While a formal assessment of Stanford might have been useful to us, it was hardly necessary. Besides, Stanford's behaviour was fairly representative of that of most adolescents with learning difficulties when they are being assessed formally. In the first place, his questionable achievement throughout his school career had led to so many formal tests that he vigorously resisted any attempts to repeat the procedure. This attitude, inevitably, contributed to a test result that was well below Stanford's true potential. Secondly, a formal, standardized procedure is simply unnecessary for this programme. Not just for Stanford, but for all adolescents of this type, a teacher needs only to examine the student's work to make an informal and quite thorough assessment of skill needs.

Stanford's needs in computing fractions are quite obvious. He is clearly able to do basic arithmetic skills, such as addition or multiplication, with comparatively little error. However, he seems to be blithely unaware of what operation to follow when computing fractions. Although he will sometimes follow the appropriate procedures for division, for example, much of the time he does not. The same is true for other operations. Stanford needs practice in the appropriate steps for computing fractions.

His writing reveals a fairly wide range of needs. Stanford shows a fairly typical profile for adolescents with learning problems. While they may be deficient in both language ability and mathematics, the former is usually comparatively worse. Among his needs in language skills are spelling, awareness of sentence structure, and proper writing of contractions. And these are just some problems in specific skills. There is also the matter of his extremely unsophisticated style and syntax, and his use of particularly awkward expressions (e.g. "like in the snow").

To see the needs for Stanford's individual programme in skill development does not require any highly specialized training. What is required is the expertise that all teachers have: the ability to examine a student's work and from it, along with an awareness of other essential factors such as the student's level of momentum (or lack of it), his pace, his behavioural profile, to determine, informally, what the objectives for that student should be.

Limiting The Objectives (Step Two)

The nature of the adolescent with learning difficulties makes this step a crucial one, and makes the teacher's role very important. From the list of needs that are identified in an informal assessment, the teacher should extract only a limited number for the student to practise in any one contract period. This is for the simple reason that the typical adolescent with learning problems, if presented with a list of *all* his obvious skill needs, is almost certainly going to indulge in avoidance behaviour. His history of failure and his lack of self-esteem make him ill-equipped to accept such a total list optimistically. Besides, most of these adolescents are already aware they have an extensive range of needs and to wave these at them is almost certain to generate resentment. It seems sensible, then, to choose a limited number of specific skills to be developed and practised in a carefully ordered sequence. This contributes to a perception on the part of the student that gains can be made. There is hope that, if his weaknesses are taken one at a time, they can be eliminated. Experience suggests that *three* skill development areas constitute the most effective number with which to deal at any one time.

The choice of the particular skills the student should practise is again another reason why the teacher is the key, for the selection should be made according to a number of criteria, not all of which appear to be immediately practical. At least one of the three choices should be a relatively easy and straightforward skill. This will reinforce the student and help him realize that there is light at the end of the tunnel. For this reason, one of the initial objectives[1] for Stanford was the proper writing of contractions. It is an achievement which takes reasonably little instruction and, likewise, reasonably little practice—an objective which can be met quickly.

Yet, the need to provide early reinforcement should not dominate the choice of objectives. Another criterion must be to work toward mastery of those skills which are of serious importance to the student. Or, to put it another way, toward overcoming those skill deficiencies which make his work appear to be substandard. For that reason, the second, and more complicated, objective for Stanford was to teach him proper sentence structure.

The third objective for Stanford was that he follow correct procedures in computing fractions. This particular element was chosen in response to a readily apparent need but, also, to another important criterion in the determination of objectives: that there be some variety in the practice work to be done. Stanford, like most adolescents with learning difficulties, in fact, like most adolescents, was easily bored. It would have been counter-productive to concentrate too exclusively in any one area.

This point leads to a fourth issue—the fact that the teacher will always determine objectives in the full awareness of a student's personality and pace of working. There are often times when this determiner alone can be the key to success or failure of the whole programme, and

[1]The use of the word "objectives" is not intended to be in the rigid technical sense; objectives, in this programme, are wider areas of improvement.

only that student's teacher is able to make this kind of decision intelligently.

Preparing the Materials For Practice (Step Three)

Once the first two stages are complete, the third step, the selection of materials, is reasonably straightforward. The type and variety of materials chosen will depend on the individual teacher's creativity and energy, and on that teacher's knowledge of commercially available products.

Generally, experience suggests that whatever the source of materials may be, the programme is most successful when these materials are self-administering; that is, when they can be completed by a student without, or with only minimal, direct supervision.

To practise his skill with fractions, Stanford was given exercises from a remedial mathematics text with the following set of steps on a card which was to be read before computing each fraction. The purpose was to make the procedure automatic.

1. *Read the fraction*
2. *Circle the sign for the operation*
3. *Repeat the rule for the operation*

Ideally, the materials used will be a *package*; that is, a specific number of exercises per objective and all of them placed in a folder, booklet, or some sort of collected unit. A variation developed by some teachers who have used this programme is to prepare a central source of practice materials. Usually a cupboard is organized to contain a range of practice materials, all indexed by type, or by level of difficulty, or both. Then, instead of having a package of his own, the student is given a list of the materials he is to complete. The student withdraws his materials from the central source as he needs them. This latter option is sometimes chosen by teachers who have a rather large number of students, and for whom, therefore, the preparation of individual packages is very demanding.

The Contract (Step Four)

Viewed in the cold light of objective analysis, the contract, as well as the progress chart, seem unnecessary elements. But teaching adolescents with learning difficulties is a special situation and often needs special elements. The contract is, in fact, a most crucial stage in this programme. Besides fulfilling the very practical element of listing what is to be done, the contract is a focus, a point of reference, for both the student and the teacher. On the contract is made specific those limited objectives which the teacher has selected. It makes concrete, for the student, the awareness of specific expectations, clear parameters, and specific goals.

For the adolescent with learning difficulties, it gives an organized structure to something that would otherwise be diffuse and fragmented. Just as the progress chart is a record of what has been accomplished, the contract is a statement of what is to be accomplished. Both elements are essential.

The structure of a contract should follow certain common-sense principles. It is important, for example, that it be simple and entirely non-threatening. The purpose is to help, not intimidate. Further, it should state the objectives, list specifically the exercises to be used for practice, and explain the relationship of these exercises to the progress chart. Here is an example of a contract which has been used successfully.

Figure 1

INDEPENDENT STUDY PROGRAMME

FOR *Stanford K... Mc...*

My objectives in this contract period are to improve my performance in the following areas:

(a) *use of contractions in written work*
(b) *show where sentences begin and end in written work*
(c) *follow function signs when computing fractions*

I will complete the following exercises during independent study time.

(a) *exercises F1 through F5 (contractions)*
(b) *exercises A1 through A15 (sentence structure)*
(c) *exercises P1 through P12 (fractions)*

Each successfully completed exercise will be initialled by my teacher.

Each successfully completed exercise is worth *one* value-point on my progress chart.

Stanford K... Mc...
Signature

Date   Teacher's Signature

Independent Study Working Time (Step Five)
Students who come to a teacher on a part-time withdrawal basis may well be spending their whole time with this teacher on an independent study programme like this. Other students who may spend a great deal of time with one teacher will probably spend only a portion of that time in independent study. In both cases, the teacher's role will be similar. The teacher will act as a monitor to ensure that all students know what they are to do, and that they do it. Ensuring a smooth operation is part of any teaching programme, independent or otherwise. Another role is that of "verifier". When a student completes an exercise, he will bring it to be initialled. But the most productive work a teacher will likely do in this time is the one-to-one tutoring of those students in most need of it.

Completing the Progress Chart (Step Six)
Experience has shown that the most sophisticated and even the most jaded of adolescents, once started on progress charts, develop a fierce pride in them. As Angelo put it, ". . . you can see what you've done." Therefore, it is vital that this aspect be conducted thoroughly, consistently, and as simply as possible. The suggested method that follows is a proven one; however, variations are certainly possible.

The progress chart in Figure 2 is a replica of Stanford's chart based on his contract from page 65. It has 25 vertical columns. Each column represents one independent study period. This particular chart anticipated that Stanford would take up to 25 independent study periods to complete his contract. However, he did not take all this time.

A single square represents *one* value-point. In the very first study period, Stanford successfully completed an exercise worth *one* value-point. He then filled in *one* square at the bottom of the first column on the left and entered the day's date. Value-points are always entered from the level achieved on the previous day. For example, on September 21 Stanford earned one value-point and the very bottom square is filled in for that day. On September 22, he again earned one value-point. He, therefore, filled in the second square from the bottom, and then filled in the column to the bottom. On September 23 he earned two value-points, filled in the third and fourth squares of the third column, and then filled in the column to the bottom. On September 25 (he was absent September 24) he earned three value points, filled in the fifth, sixth, and seventh squares of the fourth column, and filled in the column to the bottom. By entering value-points in this way, the visible evidence of progress is always in an upward and implicitly positive direction—an essential element if the chart is to contribute to a sense of achievement and momentum.

Figure 2
RECORD OF PROGRESS

Stanford K. Mc.....

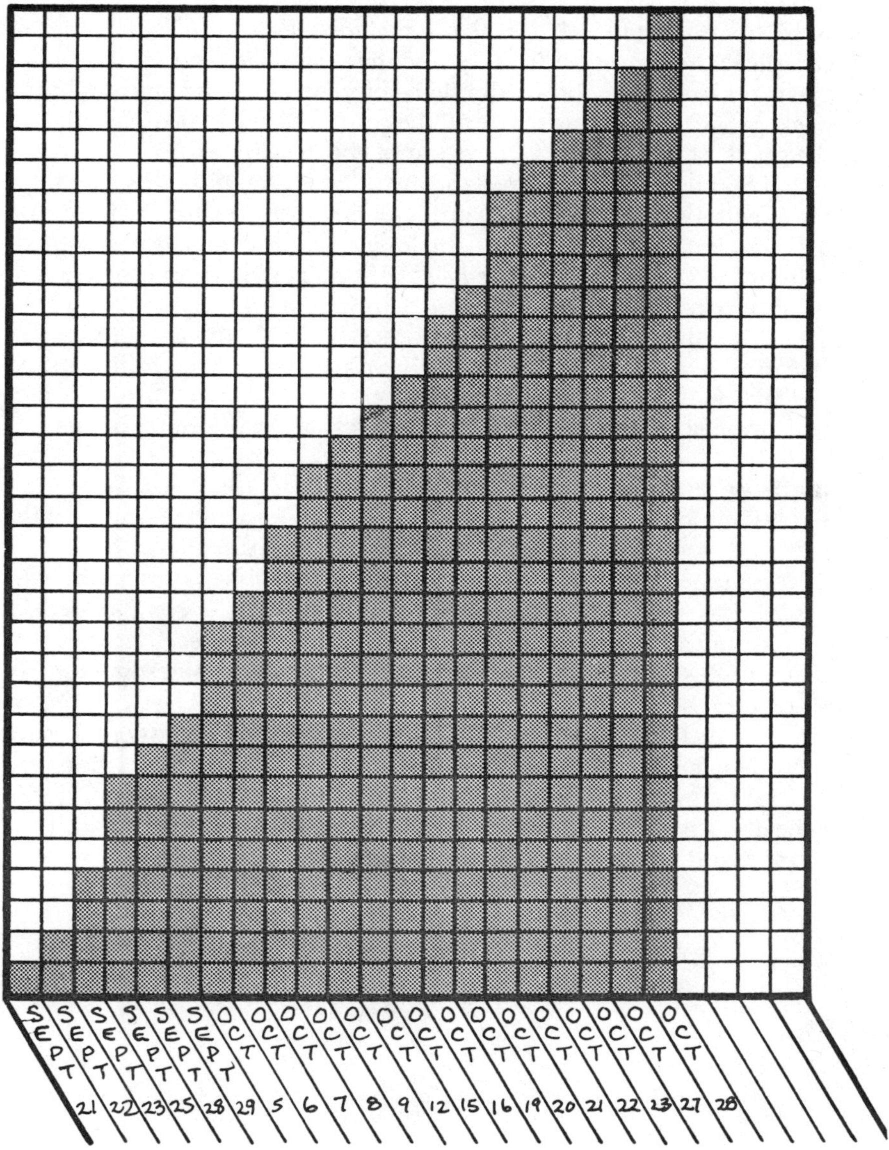

Coordination of the Progress Chart, Contract, and Learning Package

Stanford's contract calls for the completion of thirty-two practice exercises for which thirty-two value-points can be earned. Therefore, the progress chart is designed so that when one column of thirty-two squares is filled in, Stanford has reached the top. The learning package is complete; the contract is fulfilled and the chart shows this. At this point, a new package and contract should be prepared. If a student completes a package without having to use all the columns anticipated, this is all to the good. Stanford took 21 days out of the anticipated 25.

If Stanford had not earned the thirty-two value-points by the end of the twenty-fifth column, this would not have been treated as a failure on his part, but as an over-optimistic forecast on the teacher's part. More columns would have been added—ideally, more than would be necessary to complete the contract.

To summarize then, the contract will specify the number of exercises to be completed and the value-points to be earned; the learning package will contain that number of exercises; and the progress chart will provide that number of spaces for recording the value-points.

Assessing Progress and Starting a New Contract (Step Seven)

Experience has demonstrated that any kind of formal assessment at the end of a contract period is frequently counter-productive because it disrupts momentum. Furthermore, it is usually unnecessary because the teacher has been monitoring progress throughout the contract period.

In this programme, Stanford began to work at a level more consistent with his true ability. The specific objectives gave him something to work for; the structure of the programme gave him clear parameters within which to function; and his own momentum brought out some of the talent he had previously allowed to lie dormant. His work with fractions improved dramatically and immediately—as one might expect—as soon as he began to care about what he was doing. The change in his writing can be seen in the following example.

There Is A Difference Between Haste And Swiftness[1]

There are times uxen when you don't
realize you're running around like
crazy. That's haste Being swift is
rushing for a specil reason and
you know what you're doing. A persin
that rushes around alot makes mistakes
But a person that's swift does things
fast and efts ife efficent. It's
better to be a swift person than a
haste person the last kind don't win
as often.

It is readily apparent that Stanford had begun to use contractions properly, and, while his sentence structure was not perfect, it was vastly improved. Before a new contract period was begun, a decision had to be made: whether the objective of improving sentence structure should be repeated. As any teacher will quickly perceive, there was the risk of disrupting his momentum by tedious over-emphasis of the same thing. Yet, there was the equally serious risk of losing momentum by failing to reinforce the improvement already established. It is the type of decision a teacher will make frequently in this programme, and it will be made on the same basis that decisions are made for all contracts: the teacher's perception of the student's needs, personality, pace, and special requirements. In Stanford's case, it was decided that, as his momentum seemed to be solidly established and his other two objectives had been met, the sentence structure objective would be repeated in the new contract.

The cycle began again. Needs were determined and objectives established, a contract set up, a learning package prepared. And the momentum continued to be fed.

Any Questions? Or Comments?

No serious teacher would pretend that every single detail of this programme in skill development must be followed with absolute and rigid adherence. Each teacher who uses it will add a change here, a development there. That is the reality—and the beauty—of teaching. An indication of the fact that teachers modify this programme to suit their own purposes lies in the questions asked of the author over many years of presenting it in workshops. These are the questions most frequently asked.

---

[1]Stanford's interest in proverbs and pithy sayings was something he developed on his own. These expressions were not only the dominant subject of his written work, they were sprinkled throughout his conversation as well—a habit which had a remarkable effect on adults who spoke with him!

Preparing learning packages for a whole group of students seems like an awesome amount of work, isn't it? Yes, but so is most successful teaching of adolescents with learning problems. However, there is light at the end of the tunnel for teachers, too. The vast amount of commercial material available makes the task easier. Also, it is often possible to use the same exercises for a number of students. Skill needs cut a wide swath across a group of adolescents with learning problems. It is probable that several objectives will be common to a number of students, thereby reducing the amount of individual preparation necessary. Finally, the weight of preparation occurs at the point when the programme is first established. Once it is established, the students, because of such variables as individual pace and attendance patterns, tend to complete contracts intermittently rather than simultaneously. Therefore, preparation tends to become spread evenly over time as with the demands of any other teaching process.

Does computer assisted instruction have a place here—drill machines that would provide the practice exercises? Why not? Especially if a machine can relieve the teacher of the burden of preparing practice material. As long as the teacher remains in control of the programme, a machine may be a useful adjunct.

Is there not a danger that students will become bored with so much practice and therefore lose momentum? They are human and as likely to become bored as we teachers do from time to time. Part of the response lies in the choice of *three* objectives for a contract period. Variety of activity provides some relief. Another response is to vary the times when skill development periods are held. Very often, one of the objectives will be in the area of efficient thinking skills. Experience shows that activities in this area have an extremely strong appeal (see chapter 8). And, indeed, it may be productive to provide occasional relief in the form of a total but temporary departure from the structure. Fortunately, if objectives are carefully chosen, and if the teacher devotes effort to establishing and maintaining momentum, boredom is rarely a problem.

Are practice exercises the only element in a learning package? Not if the teacher feels that other elements are useful. For example, in a group of students where reading has a low value, it may be effective to grant value-points for reading a short story or a novel.

What happens to the charts when they're complete? An ideal tactic is to make them *worth* something: term marks, free time, special privileges. Attach them, with favourable comments added, to report cards. A teacher's personal ingenuity will serve well here.

When a student brings a completed exercise to the teacher for checking, must it be absolutely correct? How can it be evaluated without overly disrupting the one-to-one instruction you are doing at the time? Only teachers really understand this answer: A teacher, who has prior awareness of the objectives for a particular student, can usually skim that student's work and quickly determine whether it is essentially correct. That same teacher, who also knows the student's personality, is able to judge whether small errors should be ignored or how many errors should be ignored before the exercise requires redoing—in short, whether or not the student has grasped the principle of the exercise and has mastered it adequately. Admittedly, the process is somewhat subjective but so is much of the art of teaching.

Some of my students are very slow and will likely finish contracts well after their classmates. A student's rate and pace have usually been well established by adolescence, shaped by factors outside of school. This is not a reason to reject a programme. In fact, the variations in pace across a group can be accommodated easily in a structure like this one.

Can the variations in a group's pace be accommodated by awarding more value-points per exercise to slower students? Certainly. But this variation requires careful handling if students have a tendency to compare contracts.

When are the "meetings" to discuss contracts held? Preferably in class time—in the time regularly set aside for skill development.

Will students conduct themselves appropriately while the teacher does one-to-one instruction or "meets" with one student? Whatever behaviour patterns obtain across a group of adolescents with learning problems are likely to obtain, irrespective of whatever programmes are used. However, the author's experiences and those reported to him by colleagues suggest that management problems are in fact minimized in this type of programme.

Does it really work? Ask Stanford.

A Yawn Is A Silent Shout

Before I started this programm I was turned off. At least I sure yawned alot. That was sil sill sillently silently yelling I guess. Sometimes I wasn't exactly silent. Like the rest of the guys in this class. To tell truth we raised hell alot too. Our contracs and charts are diffrent though. When you have know were you're going you don't yawn so much, or yell either. Espech Especally when you know you're getting somewhere.

CHAPTER 6
STRUCTURING TEACHER-DIRECTED LESSONS

NOT LONG AFTER a friend of mine had assumed the directorship of a girls' training school,[1] she sought my opinion of a situation which seemed to be worsening. One of her teaching staff—the only male—while he had no teacher training, nevertheless, held an impressive set of qualifications in criminology, psychology, and counselling. Yet, one of his classes degenerated into chaos on a daily basis. Whenever my friend sat in with the class, nothing happened; whenever the teacher was alone, the roof fell in.

My own "sit-in" generated the same results at first. After the girls' initial cross-examination of me ("You a cop?" "Bet he's a narc!" "You gonna be somebody's p.o.?"[2] "What're you doin' here anyway?"), their reaction cooled to wary side glances. Not until the fourth day did my profile fade sufficiently for normal process to return.

By this time, my own convictions regarding teacher-directed lessons were beginning to crumble. The young man I was observing did not elicit answers to questions, did not encourage dialogue or discussion; he never used the chalkboard. Rather, he lectured: a complete contradiction of what I'd always believed effective. Yet the girls' acceptance of the situation, while not total, seemed reasonable enough. Until the fourth day.

At 10 a.m. the most effusive class came in for a history lesson. They entered; they sat quietly; the young man began to lecture. At 10:05 each one of the girls shifted slightly to the right in her seat and swung her left leg over her right knee, in the aisle. The teacher winced but continued. At precisely 10:08 all the girls pulled the hems of their skirts to just above their knees. The young man compensated by shifting the aim of his lecture

[1]a prison-cum-school for juvenile offenders given specific sentences by the courts; the term "training school" is no longer in vogue.

[2]probation officer

to a point on the back wall, well above their heads. At 10:10 the skirts went to mid-thigh, and the lecture went higher up the wall. At 10:12 the skirts went higher, and so did the direction of the lecture. By 10:15 the teacher was, quite literally, lecturing to the ceiling!

At this point, the girls began to walk around and chat with each other. One lit a cigarette. Another made herself comfortable at the warm air register and went to sleep. Two of them began to play with a tattered deck of cards. The situation, in teaching terms, was an unmitigated disaster. Before long, the young man simply shrugged his shoulders at me, sat down at his desk, and began to read.

Like so many predicaments involving the adolescent with learning problems, this one was both funny and sad. It was also unnecessary. Although responsibility for the incident must ultimately rest with the teacher's techniques of management, there is no question that part of the problem was that he chose to lecture to a group for whom the method was highly inappropriate.

The lecture as a teaching technique for these students has little to recommend it. Attending to a lecture demands an unstinting willingness to play the game of "school". The listeners must acknowledge that the material is worth their while; they must relinquish the right to questioning and argument; and they must make, on their own, the connections between the lecture and previously-learned information. These factors are not necessarily beyond the competence of adolescents with learning difficulties; it's just that the majority of them will not play the game this way.

The lecture technique can be successful on occasion, particularly when a lecture demonstration is in order. Certainly, a brief lecture on a reasonably simple point can be very efficient. There are even times when a teacher might use the lecture as a technique for building students' self-esteem, for the method does have an air of scholarship about it—albeit somewhat pretentious. Nevertheless, adolescents with learning problems are an unlikely audience for even the infrequent use of the lecture technique. Fortunately, very few of their teachers use it.

A greater number, however, use a technique that is not all that dissimilar: duplicated sheets of "work" that are distributed at the beginning of class with the instruction to work quietly and independently; and that may or may not be discussed at the end of class. While this method may have a surface validity and, from time to time, an immediate appeal to the students depending upon the interest-generating capacity of the material, its long-range impact is likely to be counterproductive. In the first place, it is usually fragmenting in its effect, as the various pieces of paper are not always connected in theme or purpose.

More serious is the atmosphere of filling in time that the practice creates and the impression fostered among the students that they are unable to work with textbooks and notebooks like "normal" students. Not that sheets of "work" cannot be effective. However, to be truly productive, independent practice activities must be part of a coordinated and cohesive programme, i.e. with a contract, a progress chart, and a clear sense of meeting individual needs.

Both the lecture method and the indiscriminate work-sheet method are chosen, mistakenly, on the premise that they are effective in maintaining classroom control. As well, they may be chosen because of the belief that the traditional lesson style in which the teacher questions, directs, stimulates, and provokes—part of the real *fun* of teaching—just does not work with these students.

Not so. Teacher-directed lessons can be just as effective for adolescents with learning difficulties as for those without. Granted, the impact of a lesson will always be affected by the amount and quality of preparation, the subject, the teacher's own personality, the class mood, the time of day—all the variables that can make the process so exciting. Yet, unless they experience some teacher-directed lessons, these adolescents will miss part of the real delight and excitement in learning. For, in this style of lesson, there is reasoning, argument, exchange of ideas, divergent thinking, challenge—all of which could take place without a teacher, but are guaranteed by the presence of a teacher who has prepared.

Ideally, the teacher's role in this technique is that of initiator and, then, of spontaneous director—a chairperson who guides and shapes the lesson toward a specific objective. Ideally, again, it is a technique that builds rapport among the students of a group and between teacher and students. The impression should be generated that the particular teacher and the particular students are a unit. A sense of membership in a unit (i.e. the "my class" phenomenon to both teacher and student), in turn, strengthens the rapport, and makes teaching easier, learning more pleasant, and classroom management a matter of reduced concern.

The fact that this ethos does not always develop in classes of adolescents with learning problems is probably attributable to their collective negative experiences. A history of failure, lack of self-esteem, and the absence of momentum build a wall of distrust, cynicism, rejection, and behaviour problems. It is an intimidating wall for a teacher to encounter. The temptation to lecture or use independent work sheets is attractive, for both methods seem to offer less risk of potential disorder. Yet, the benefits that attach to the experience of teacher-directed lessons are worth the risk. If the preparation is careful and thorough, if the approach is sensible, and if the teacher keeps the perspective of his audience in mind, the technique can be extremely effective.

For adolescents who have difficulty learning, there seem to be certain constants that will make a teacher-directed lesson more effective. And who better to voice these constants than the students themselves?

The statements that follow were solicited from one of my classes. I was preparing to teach a summer "refresher" course to teachers of these students, and to generate some discussion material for the course, I invited the students to compose a set of rules that they would like all teachers to follow. Here, typeset, but otherwise unaltered, are the results. They make one wonder just what a learning problem really is!

These Are The Rules

With best wishes to Mr Weber's teaching class from (3-4) 9G

1. *Always give time to unnderstand the thing your at before you go to the next thing. Students get two, three steps behind and then its too late.*

   Glen M.

2. *Give enough triles and exampls of the thing you're at to make sure everyones got it. Especilly those guys that dont understand it all at first.*

   Freddy Mc.

3. *Tell your students what the class is all about before you start. Its easer to understand a class when the teacher says up front whats going to happen.*

   Brian W.

4. *All teachers talk too much. Don't. When your talking we can't tell you what's going on in our heads.*

   Russell "The Stosh" V.

5. *Make sure your student's heads are clear of the last class and really into your class before you start something important.*

   Enzo O. and Jules F.

6. *When you give work after the lesson part give your students time in class to work on it and then stick around and dont go off to the lounge or someplace like that because its easier to do stuff if you know the teachers there to help if you get stuck.*

   Ben R. Robin F. Mark H.

7. *Use the [chalk]board. Its always easier to see things instead of hearing a hole bunch of words.*

   Little Richard W.

8. *Don't put surprises in the homework. Stuff that works out in class is always easy. Then the homework has a few easy ones and all of a sudden a hard one that we weren't taught how to do. That's why kids dont do homework much.*

   "Hump" McV.

9. *Don't make too big a deal about everything. Every teacher thinks their subject is the most important thing in the world. Lunch period is.*

Anonimus

10. *Put yourself in your students shoes when you do your lessons. We don't always think like you do.*

Paul A and Ernie Y.

9G could certainly have mounted an effective, if somewhat unorthodox, seminar all by themselves. Although their rules waver occasionally from straight advice on lesson presentation into educational philosophy, their prescriptions are hallmarks of reason. Essentially, their rules can be summarized to show that, for them, an effective teacher-directed lesson is one with clear direction and purpose, one for which both students and teacher are prepared, one that proceeds with clear sequence and appropriate pace, that provides opportunity for guided practice, and that is part of an overall plan. These students are not interested in episodic, *ad hoc* lessons.

What follows is a suggested plan for organizing teacher-directed lessons. Of course, there will be variations from teacher to teacher and from class to class, but these six steps seem to respond to the stated concerns of the students.

Steps In a Teacher-Directed Lesson

1. Focussing

When a teacher begins a lesson, he has had the benefit of preparing the lesson, working with it, rearranging it—he knows what he is about. The students, on the other hand, are intellectually and emotionally in a variety of different places when a lesson begins. They need to be brought together or put in a state of readiness for the instruction that will follow. A teacher-directed lesson must accommodate and plan for this need. There must be some brief activity that will generate an anticipation on the part of the students and a focus on the topic to follow. The activity might take the form of a brief review of yesterday's lesson, if today's is an extension of it. It might be a brief soliciting of students' knowledge of the subject of the lesson about to follow. It may be a few number facts, if the lesson is one in mathematics. It may be the presentation of a statistic, if the lesson is in social studies, or a figure of speech, if the lesson is in poetry. It may be the presentation of a proverb or saying, if the lesson is to be interpretive reading. For every lesson, there is an unlimited source of possibilities. All that is necessary is that the device be brief, simple, and attractive enough to focus attention.

2. Statement of Purpose (Objective)
This step is a simple communication from the teacher to the students about the purpose of what is to follow. Such a statement is a bridge from the focussing to the instruction itself. It also shows the students what to expect and conveys to them that the teacher regards the whole process as mature and mutually respectful interchange. Like focussing, this step should be a brief one. It is not the time for a grand exposition of educational philosophy.[1]

3. Presentation of Material
Although adolescents with learning problems can encounter snags at any point in a lesson, this stage, *Presentation of Material,* and the next, *Instruction,* seem to hold the greatest number of pitfalls. This is because both stages require so much to be manipulated simultaneously. It follows then that these stages must be planned most carefully, with a constant awareness of the perspective, rate of assimilation, and pace which these students are likely to demonstrate in a lesson.

> *While this chapter was being written, I observed one of my student teachers present a lesson to a group of adolescents in a special education class. It was a social studies class called "Contemporary Topics" and the subject was land reform in Central America.*
>
> *My student was a pleasure to observe. She was already a fine teacher, for she enhanced thorough planning and an instinctive awareness of her audience with a cheery disposition. Yet, a simple omission in her presentation of material caused me to experience what many a learning problem adolescent must go through.*
>
> *She had chosen San Salvador as an example and she had obviously done her homework. There were maps, charts, and a simple graph on the chalkboard. She had taught two prior lessons on the arithmetic involved, a lesson on map reading, and now she was building neatly on the responses from the class. But she had not identified San Salvador on the wall map of Central America to which she frequently referred. I am embarrassed to admit I did not know which country was San Salvador. Since this information was crucial to the lesson, I became totally bewildered and had fallen several steps behind. One of my colleagues in the special education class (by now, they were my colleagues) rescued himself and me with a ques-*

[1]The tongue is only partly in cheek. Note Russell V.'s Rule #4.

tion that reflected both his respect of the teacher and his depth of frustration.

"Please, miss. Excuse me. Where the hell is San Salvador?"

Students need all the basic information before the instruction built on it can be effective. Glen M. put it well in Rule #1. If students fall two or three steps behind, it is often too late.

4. Instruction

The crux of a lesson is at the point where the information and skills and materials are brought together to meet the purpose stated in Step 2. Sometimes, this will be accomplished by careful eliciting of responses from the students. Occasionally, it will be done by a demonstration. Sometimes, an issue will be presented to students to pursue independently and then a collective effort will be coordinated by the teacher and brought to a conclusion. Whatever the method, once the instruction or the gain in new knowledge has been established, it is essential that there be adequate, immediate reinforcement (Rule #2). Frequently, the complete instructional phase will have to be repeated. If more examples or duplicate material are available, these should be introduced, but only if the examples reinforce the learning experience precisely. This is not the time for surprises (Rule #8).

There is a horrid term in special education that has some utility here: overlearning. Adolescents with problems need the reinforcement that comes with repetition and frequent trials until they achieve a level of confidence. It is not that these students lack ability; it is that we rarely see the ability they have. And that is a factor of confidence. A confident student expends effort and works to potential. A student with a poor self-image does not.

5. Guided Practice

Rule #6 may be the cynical reflection of personal experience, but its presence on the list can likewise be accounted for by the factor of confidence. There is no better resource for reinforcement than the teacher who made the original presentation. Thus, having given the instruction, the teacher should circulate while the students are working on further examples of the concept. The mere presence of the teacher adds to their confidence and, thereby, to their degree of effort. But the usefulness of guided practice is more concrete than that. To be confident that they have "got it", students need to practise on their own. With the teacher present, they can receive the help or clarification immediately, before the all-too-frequent rejection response of the adolescent with learning problems sets in. Time and opportunity for guided practice must be built into the plan for every teacher-directed lesson.

6. Homework

"Normal" students get homework, and not to give homework to their "problem" colleagues is doing them a disservice. Acknowledging their predilection to avoidance, however, the teacher will find it useful to plan so that this stage will be included initially in the time allowed for *Guided Practice.* The fact that adolescents with learning problems are afraid of homework is a substantial factor in their avoidance of it. Doing homework with the teacher present not only circumvents the disciplinary consequences, it also provides a means for confidence to grow. Once the students have developed a sense of confidence and acquired the habit of doing homework, then this stage becomes simply that part of the lesson done at home.

Finally, "Hump" McV's admonition in Rule #8 is certainly worth a teacher's consideration. It is distressing enough to fail; it is far more distressing to perceive that failure as provoked by inadequate planning or deliberate obfuscation.

Using the Chalkboard (and other illustrative aids)

There are so many advantages to simultaneous visual and auditory instruction that it is difficult to believe that all teachers do not use a chalkboard (or equivalent) all the time. Students can see a concept build on the chalkboard as the lesson progresses; the teacher can use the design for summary, for reinforcement, even for speedy re-teaching, if necessary. A chalkboard outline enables the teacher to return easily to stages already covered in the lesson, if he perceives that certain students have become confused. There is opportunity to illustrate comparisons and contrasts and to isolate visually what is most important. A chalkboard outline reduces dependence on the short-term and long-term memory. It can provide a source for note-taking, contributing to a sense of cumulative achievement—something adolescents with learning difficulties do not experience very often. In short, the chalkboard is not just a useful aid in a teacher-directed lesson; it is a necessary one.

The Matter of Teacher Behaviour and Student Behaviour in Teacher-Directed Lessons

Of the three main "voices" in a typical lesson, those of the teacher, the material, and the students, the last voice should ideally be the strongest. If the purpose of such a lesson is to provoke original thought, stimulate the exchange of ideas, encourage evaluation and analysis, increase awareness, promote listening and oral skills, then it stands to reason that the students should do as much of the thinking, conjecturing, debating, and listening as is possible. The teacher has done all this while preparing the lesson; during the lesson, it is the students' turn. The teacher's role should be that of discussion leader, a chairperson who stimulates and directs the interchange, receives and redirects the responses, keeps the discussion moving, and intervenes only when necessary. This, of course, is the ideal. Reality, in classes for adolescents with learning difficulties, is often very much at odds with the ideal.

In part, this occurs because of the disruptive behaviour patterns in a class of these students. Certainly, some of this disruptive behaviour is deliberate: avoidance techniques that will divert revelation of ignorance and inability. Some of it is instinctive. There are a few students who simply do not know how to conduct themselves in the group dialogue that occurs in a teacher-directed lesson. If one follows these students to the schoolyard, the cafeteria, and the street, one will see exactly the same behaviour where a group situation obtains. Nevertheless, unproductive behaviour patterns are not sufficient reason for a teacher to dismiss the benefits of the teacher-directed lesson technique. Besides, these patterns are entirely within a teacher's power to control. If students have begun to develop a sense of their own momentum and if they are confident of intellectual and emotional safety in their classroom, knowing that their opinions, their conjectures, and their ideas will be respected by their teacher, disruptive behaviour patterns will diminish.

Not infrequently, disadvantages that show up in the technique are the product of the material being used as the focus of the lesson. Teachers of adolescents with learning problems know that boredom rears its head quickly—again, the problem of avoidance, but also of cultural and socio-economic background and, most particularly, of the unwillingness to play the game of school. The response to this phenomenon is inevitably a search for material that is "relevant". A reasonable reaction indeed; yet, relevance alone is not enough. No matter how relevant the material, it must be packaged in a way that will contribute to a sense of incremental gains and, thereby, to a development of momentum. Teachers of English or reading will often find a "relevant" novel that, theoretically, should excite students' interest. Sometimes, it does, but the sheer size and effort implied by a full-length novel is often too intimidating. The same objectives can be accomplished by thematically connected pieces of prose that are not only relevant, but short. Subjects like mathematics or social studies seem to have an easier road to relevance: e.g. daily reported sports data to practise computing skills; real revolutions or border wars for practice in map reading skills or economic and political analysis. Yet, these subjects, too, must be packaged in manageable units to be effective. Organization of the material is easily as important as its relevance.

Ultimately, however, for the success of a teacher-directed lesson, the teacher is the key. It is the teacher who organizes the material; it is the teacher who creates the sense of safety, who makes it known that all persons and their opinions are respected; and, above all, it is the teacher who shapes and controls the pace and flow of a lesson. In the teacher-directed technique, this is achieved by the art of asking questions and responding to answers.

> *Stanford (see Chapter 5) turned to his vast store of proverbs and pithy sayings, one day, to offer me this very useful observation. It was Careers Day at our school, and I had the happy task of talking about teaching. Even though my students had little hope—or desire—of completing the academic requirements for a teaching career, they showed up loyally at my session.*
>
> *When the discussion eventually turned to teaching styles, Stanford contributed thusly: "I know why you like teaching so much sir! Because even though you don't know all the answers, you get to ask the questions!"*

I suspect that he had dipped into James Thurber for that one. Irrespective of the source, he had hit on a vital issue. Teachers ask the questions in a lesson, and on their questioning techniques a lesson can stand or fall.

Certainly, there are absolutes in the art of questioning. A teacher will deliberately involve everyone in a teacher-directed lesson, even those who are not volunteering answers; questions must be clear in their content and in their intent; they will often be tailored in difficulty to the type of student being asked; it seems more useful to ask questions which generate developed answers rather than yes/no answers. All teachers are familiar with this advice. For lessons with adolescents who have learning problems, there is additional food for thought.

There seems to be, in teacher-directed lessons, a very strong tradition in which the "good" user of this technique is perceived as dynamic. No one would argue with the logic of this. But, in the translation of dynamism into technique, there seems to have developed a concomitant tradition that questioning must always be in rapid-fire style. Otherwise, the lesson is not dynamic. The point is apparent not just from empirical evidence; it is supported by research.[1] To be sure, there are times in a teacher-directed lesson when rapid-fire questioning is productive and stimulating. But for adolescents with learning problems, the pitfalls of the style tend to outweigh the long-term advantages.

Research shows that teachers allow an average of one second of "pondering-time" before repeating the question, asking another one, or singling out a student. Not only does this brief time over-challenge the

---

[1]Rowe, M.B., *The Reading Teacher, XXXIV*, November, 1980, pp. 143-46. (The article also reviews literature on this point.)

slower thinker, it often precludes the possibility of higher level thinking—the kind of thinking that takes longer, no matter what the ability of the student. In effect, it appeals to the facile-tongued and the facile-witted, and very few adolescents with problems are in this category. It also tends to force both teacher and students into the mould of dull, content-only questioning, the kind of tedium that can cause disruptive behaviour.

Another pitfall is that the rapid-fire style tends to generate the worst of all possible outcomes: an ethos in which the students relate only to the teacher, not to each other. Inevitably, they begin to play "guess-what-is-in-teacher's-mind" or "guess-what-teacher-wants". Still more serious, the teacher himself begins to play this way. An extension of this often grows from the teacher's genuine wish to reinforce with an immediate "Good!" "Right!" "Yes!". Unfortunately, this kind of verbal reward, if offered immediately, cuts off further thinking.

Students who have a history of learning more slowly or with more difficulty need more time to think. They also need, because of their all-too-frequent poverty of expressive skills, more time to answer. Teachers of these students must pay attention to these needs for more time, even if it appears to be at the sacrifice of dynamism. It is a matter, once again, of the teacher's adjusting to the nature of students who do not learn at the customarily accepted pace. Sometimes, the adjustment is difficult for both teacher and students. The dividends, however, are usually worth the shift in gears. Proper pacing and proper spacing of clear, effective questions can stimulate high-level thinking and, surely, that must be a long-range purpose of every teacher-directed lesson.

A Contribution to Momentum

Teacher-directed lessons will form only part of the catalogue of methods a teacher will use. But, like other techniques, this one can be instrumental in generating and maintaining momentum. The key, as always, is the teacher. By planning and structuring the presentations for these special students, a teacher not only helps to build their sense of progress, but also builds rapport. Adolescents with learning problems need that rapport: the interchange, the role-modelling, and the experience of a trustful group relationship with an adult figure. The most available figures in their lives, other than their families, are their teachers, and one of the most effective ways to build that relationship in a classroom is through the teacher-directed style.

CHAPTER 7

STRUCTURING GROUP-DISCUSSION LESSONS

April 9, 1978

Memorandum to: *W.T. Ass't. Supt.*
From: *Sister Frances M., Principal*
Subject: *Probationary Teacher — Scott St. C.*

Further to your request of March 13, the final report concerning Mr. St. C.'s work with the adjusted behavioral class E-24 will be submitted by the end of May, in order that you may arrange for his permanent contract, appropriate salary increases, etc. etc.

In the meantime, I'm delighted to state yet again that his success with E-24 has been an example to us all. The constant low-grade "violence" which characterized E-24 has all but disappeared; I rarely see them on disciplinary matters, and outbursts of the kind to which we had previously been accustomed seem to have ended. Mr. St. C. is a gifted teacher. We are pleased to have him on the staff.

The memo is real. So is the assistant superintendent, the principal, Scotty St. C.—and E-24. Concern for the latter group was what each of them shared; E-24 was an experimental group of young adolescents who, in another time and place, would probably have been institutionalized because of their extreme and unacceptable behaviour. Instead, because of a far-seeing administration, they were brought together for one last try in the regular school system. Their core teacher, Scotty, had been a student teacher of mine, one of those naturally able persons whose teaching ability lends support to the conviction that teacher training really only polishes the skills that are inherent in the first place. Scotty showed himself to be made of stern stuff, too—fortunately for him, because E-24 almost terminated his career before it had properly begun.[1]

---

[1]It is a curious anomaly in the teaching profession that the most difficult tasks inevitably are put in the hands of the most young and inexperienced teachers. One prefers to believe that the practice is a vote of confidence in their youth and energy. Still, one wonders what would happen if the same practice obtained in, say, neurosurgery?

But he lasted. So did they. And both triumphed. In the following year, all but one of E-24 were successfully integrated into regular classes.

To attribute this positive outcome wholly to any one factor would hardly be accurate. There were many reasons for the success. But, in Scotty's own *post facto* analysis of the accomplishment, he pointed out that the single thing of which he was most proud was that he had taught the members of E-24 to talk. Not just verbalize, for that they did to excess in any case; rather, he had taught them to *talk to* and *with* one another; to talk to other people in the school, especially those in authority; he had taught them to articulate their grievances and their concerns, to ask questions, to listen, to rely on persuasion over physical force. In short, Scotty had led them toward the gift of oral fluency and all the attributes, both intellectual and behavioural, that come with it.

Oral Fluency and Group Discussion Lessons: Why Bother?

Every teacher of adolescents with learning problems bears witness to the emotional frustrations that grow from their being unable to express themselves adequately. These students are often physical in their communication because they lack the ability to express themselves in words or, at least, they are not accustomed to approaching the solution of a problem by communicating verbally. Very often, the negative social behaviour of adolescents with learning problems is a direct outgrowth of their never having considered verbal communication as a possibility. These students not only need to learn *how* to communicate effectively in words, they also need to learn that the option exists and can make a difference.

Speech habits not only help to shape social behaviour, they help to shape the entire personality of the individual—his attitude, his presentation of self, and the form and quality of his interaction with the environment.

Just as crucial is the influence of good speech on thinking. One's ability to use the language is inseparably linked to the quality of one's thought processes. It is moot to consider how often these students fail to utilize inherent qualities of originality, perception, and analysis simply because they lack the means of expression.This is a point with which teachers can be sympathetic for we too suffer the same frustration from time to time. The major difference between us and our students is that for most of them the problem is relatively constant.

Strangely, the difficulty most teachers face in making the decision to give importance to oral communication is more ethical than pedagogical. It has been well-established that significant numbers of adolescents with learning difficulties come from cultures and from socio-economic groups where effective oral communication is not a high priority nor even very highly valued. Does a teacher have the right, much less the responsibility, to attempt to modify his students' speech patterns? The nagging doubt is often reinforced by students who resist attempts to improve their speech by arguing that their present level of communication is understood at home, on the street, on the job. Perhaps, a reasonable answer is in J.H. Newsom's report to the British government in 1963:

> *We simply do not know how many people are frustrated in their lives by inability ever to express themselves adequately; or how many never develop intellectually because they lack the words to think and reason. This is a matter as important to economic life as it is to personal living; industrial relations as well as marriages come to grief on failures in communication.*[1]

The answer is supported by the Speech Association of America's statement in the same year:

> *Speaking is prerequisite to the development of a sense of identity. Speech habits are important to vocational success and effective citizenship. Speech is thus central to the nature of humankind, to the development of the person, and to the functioning of political, economic, and social institutions.*[2]

Surely both statements are sufficient justification for a programme that emphasizes oral communication, for it is this skill that makes everything else in the educational process useful.

What are the Objectives?

For some time and with considerable success, sociologists, psychologists, and linguists have been detailing what is wrong with the oral fluency of the majority of those adolescents who are likely to be identified as having learning difficulties. Regrettably, they have done moderately little to suggest means of correcting the problem. Research confirms what was already empirically evident in the classroom, but any guidance toward remediating the matter is rarely forthcoming. The teacher is left to his own devices.

Nevertheless, the research can be very useful to the classroom teachers' planning, for it has pinpointed the areas on which a teacher might concentrate in a programme to develop oral fluency. Bernstein was one of the first to point out what he called the "elaborated code" of the fluent and the "restricted code" of the dysfluent; how the former is explicit and attempts to explain fully, whereas the latter tends to assume rather than render his dialogue. The "elaborated code" speaker is

---

[1]Newsom, J.H., *Half Our Future*, H.M.S.O. Report, 1963.

[2]"The Field of Speech: Its Purposes and Scope in Education", Speech Association of America, 1963.

flexible, varied, confident, tends to use the subjunctive mood when appropriate, is respectful, and tends to request rather than command. The "restricted code" user is rigid, imperative, brusque, and attends poorly. He listens poorly and offends with rudeness that, ironically, is not always intended.

Others like Lawton and Troike and Abrahams have shown the close correlation of dysfluency with lower socio-economic class and have made clear the lack of importance generally attributed to articulate speech by this group. Most people are familiar with the impressive work of Vygotsky who showed how interwoven are speech and quality of thought.

From the work of people like this and from their own empirical observations, teachers are able to extract information from which to form objectives for their lessons. Essentially, the objectives of these lessons are subsumed in two major points: (1) given the nature and personal history of students with learning difficulties, it is fundamental to establish an awareness of the value and importance of good speech; (2) once the student begins to appreciate the significance of fluent oral speech to his life, the next stage is to work on its development. These two objectives are the foundation of an effective programme, coupled with the pedagogical reality that opportunities to improve oral speech must be structured by the teacher and that improvement is likely to occur only if there are sufficient opportunities to practise. What follows is a series of suggestions for establishing a programme to promote oral fluency.

Suggestion One: Creating the Atmosphere: Tapping the Potential

One of the initial problems with which teachers of adolescents must deal is making their students use the communication abilities they have already. Students with learning difficulties will often deliberately mask their true speech capabilities with slang, mispronunciations, and grammatical crudities to emphasize the clear distinction between themselves and the rest of the world. Poor speech seems to be a declared badge of membership in the specific peer culture. This selection, for example, came from Ivan, aged 15. It is a response he made in an English class for slower learners, where his peers were listening and, apparently, the mask was important.

> *"Like-uh-uh-like-well, like Charley, he was always takin' it in the ear, like. Like he's kinda dumb anyways and th'others they always-uh-uh-they always like treat him like a retard, see?"*

The above was accompanied with a great deal of aimless physical movement. There was no eye contact during the response which was delivered in a monotone.

Most teachers are aware that admonitions against such levels of language use are of little avail. Sermonizing is counter-productive.

Exercises (i.e. "Correct the mistakes in numbers one through ten."), teachers know from experience, have almost no effect on their students' speech. Yet, the irony is that most students with learning difficulties have better speech than they customarily use.

This is Ivan, no less than one hour later. The situation has changed to an auto repair class. When the passage was recorded,[1] he was leaning over the engine of an exhausted 1967 Chevrolet, debating with a classmate who faced him from the other side.

> *"OK! OK! But no carburetor's gonna last long like this! You gotta do an overhaul or else get a new one but you can't put this dumb thing back on!"*

Ivan's "school speech" is like that of most adolescents. When the situation is natural, that is, free of the constraints imposed by peer pressure or by self consciousness, when interest is high, and when the purpose is clear, the quality of oral communication rises toward potential. The key for the teacher, then, seems to be to organize situations in which these elements obtain. Well thought-out group discussion lessons are ideal.

A group discussion enables more students to talk more of the time. It removes much of the artificial barrier that many students feel when they perceive that their speech is being monitored by their peers and by their teacher. In short, it is perhaps the most natural of situations for speaking. Thus, if it is well organized and structured to achieve a clear purpose and, if the material to be discussed is even remotely interesting, a teacher can be reasonably assured that useful dialogue will take place.

Suggestion Two: Structuring the Groups

The ideal number of participants in a group seems to be five. Four will work—not as well; so will six, but these are the outer limits. Thus, a teacher's rule of thumb in establishing groups is to aim for five participants.

The teacher should appoint students to a particular group. To suggest to a class of adolescents with learning problems that they spontaneously form their own groups will lead to unnecessary confusion, embarrassment, and, sometimes, even arguments. Students would rather be told where and with whom to form a group. Not only is this more efficient—they start working more quickly—it also relieves them of the social responsibility of deciding with whom to group. The strongest advantage, however, is that, by taking the responsibility for placing people in groups, the teacher can organize combinations of students for

---

[1]Both this passage and the one taken from the English class were recorded on tape as part of a larger study. The students had agreed to the study and the fact that they would not be told when taping would occur. On neither occasion was Ivan aware that he was being recorded.

maximum effect. There are times when the most able students and the least able should be spread evenly among the groups in the class. There are times when these students might gain more by being grouped together. At other times, the most verbal and the least verbal might gain from being grouped together, respectively. There are infinite varieties and combinations, and only the teacher, with the perspective he has, is able to organize the groups for the students' maximum benefit.

Suggestion Three: Teaching the Groups to Function

Despite the fact that it seems normal for five people to work as a group when they are brought together for a specific purpose, it does not always work out that way. Very often, one person will dominate while another will be submissive and silent. Still another may not co-operate. Needless to say, with adolescents who have learning difficulties, the potential for these problems is high. Teachers who have abandoned the group discussion technique have often done so because the student groups simply did not work as groups. Therefore, an essential step in establishing this technique is to teach students how to work as a group. Experience has shown that methods like the following are ideal for this.

Students are presented with a problem for which there is a reasonably straightforward answer. However, for the solution to be achieved, every member of the group must contribute and co-operate. If even one fails to do so, the group will not produce the answer.

In the following task, for example, all members of the group receive this information:

The ODDO Board of Directors Meeting

From across the world, six owners of large duck ranches have come together to hold the second meeting of an organization called ODDO (Organization of Domestic Duck Owners). Each person is from a different country. Each represents all the domestic duck owners in his or her country.

At their first meeting, they agreed that each of them would be able to cast one vote for every one million domestic ducks in his or her country. At this second meeting, they must decide how many votes each country should have in ODDO.

Mr. Postma, for example, who is from The Netherlands, will be able to cast three votes since there are three million ducks in his country. Ms Velasquez from Colombia will be able to cast fewer votes than Mr. Postma because Colombia has fewer domestic ducks than The Netherlands.

Fortunately, all six people are honest and anxious to co-operate so it should be possible for them to figure out how many votes each is allowed.

The members of your own group are official recorders for ODDO. You are to publish the minutes of this second meeting. The minutes should include the name of each board member, what country each is from, and how many votes each is able to cast.

Each member of the group also receives one additional piece of information. These additional pieces, when shared co-operatively and considered with the basic information, will lead quite easily to a specific answer. Student number 1, for example, receives this:

Duck owners in Japan are very proud of a new breed of domestic duck they have developed. In fact, the owner representing Japan knows that he will have more votes to cast than the owners from at least three of the other countries. He is not too sure about Italy because the owner who represents that country has told him that, since the first board meeting, Italy has doubled its population of domestic ducks. This means that only the host country for this meeting has more domestic ducks than Italy.

This information is held by #2:

On the night before the meeting, Mr. Stephenson, from the host country, held a dinner for the other owners. Each person brought gifts for the others from his or her home country. Everyone was delighted with Mr. Tanaka's Japanese puppets, especially Mrs. Benelli, who gave everyone a beautiful ivory model of the leaning tower of Pisa, one of Italy's most famous attractions.

Number 3 has this:

Miss Olandu missed the opening ceremonies because the plane she took from her ranch in Nigeria had engine trouble over Quebec. However, she is not too worried because she realizes that duck ranching is a new idea in Nigeria and hers will be the smallest vote anyway. Nigeria has only half as many ducks as Colombia, for example. Miss Olandu was surprised to learn that Italy and Japan had the same number of ducks because she had thought that Japan's population was larger.

Four holds these facts:

Because there are only half as many domestic ducks in Colombia as in Italy, Ms Velasquez is interested in discussing an exchange programme with one of the larger producers like Italy or, perhaps, Canada. During the discussion at the dinner given by Mr. Stephenson, she learned that Canada has a million more ducks than Japan and would be very happy to discuss a programme.

Student #5 holds the completing details:

Mr. Postma is somewhat worried about a problem with the duck population in Holland. It seems that disease is killing off the breeding stock there and owners are having serious difficulties. At the first meeting of ODDO, Holland had one million more ducks than Italy. Now, at the second meeting, he has learned that although every other country's duck population has increased since that meeting, Holland's has remained exactly the same.

Because tasks like these have a clear purpose, because experience proves them to be of high interest, and because they require co-operative verbal interchange in a natural group setting, students take to them eagerly, and most of the time their commitment to solving the problem is genuine. A teacher can, therefore, use this experience productively, to have his students consider just how a group functions. In an after-the-fact analysis, an assessment of why the group succeeded or failed in reaching a solution, students can be led to examine factors like the need to listen to one another, the value of clarity in making a point, the advantages of having someone act as group leader, or the benefits of a systematic approach. Above all, they can be made to see the wisdom of talking to and with one another for a common purpose.

The process is always one of the teacher's structuring situations to establish momentum. Once students realize and accept the importance of each individual in a group and, moreover, the importance of each individual's contribution to the group, the level of oral language rises naturally to potential. As well, once students accept the idea and purpose of group discussions, then the teacher's periodic interventions to modify and improve speech patterns are more acceptable.

Obviously, no teacher is going to abandon the curriculum to devote all energies to problems like "The ODDO Board of Directors Meeting"; however, this type of problem, when served up occasionally, has great value in refuelling momentum, particularly if it is used to demonstrate the practical value of clear, co-operative dialogue. Naturally, the benefit lies in the *post facto* analysis of the group's attempt to solve a problem more than in the problem itself.

With certain groups, it may be necessary to provide easier problems or problems which, on the surface at least, appear less imposing. Here is an example. All students in the group are given this information:

The Joggers

Every morning, Tom, Reggie, and Jim go jogging together. Although they are very good friends, there is quite a difference in their ages. One of them is close to retirement and another is only in his early thirties.

The problem is to figure out who is the oldest and who is the youngest.

Each individual member is given additional information as follows:

#1 Tom is a bachelor.
#2 The oldest person has a son who plays tennis.
#3 Reggie is not the youngest person.
#4 Reggie's salary is the smallest of the three.
#5 The oldest person has the largest income.

Suggestion Four: The *Post Facto* Analysis
All teachers have their own techniques for activities like this. Nevertheless, the following questions offer a useful beginning for students to consider how their group functioned. Ideally, these questions would be discussed by each group in the class immediately after the attempt at the problem.

1. Did our group have a leader? What are the advantages of having a leader?
2. Did anyone not contribute information necessary to solving the problem? OR Was anyone reluctant to contribute necessary information? OR Was necessary information contributed but not heard by the rest of the group? If the answer is yes to any of the above, try to find out why. How can the problems above be avoided?
3. Did the group become involved in discussing material of no importance to the problem? Why?
4. Did anyone in the group misunderstand what another person was trying to say? If the answer is yes, try to find out why.
5. Make a list of at least three things your group will try to do next time.

Suggestion Five: Follow-up is Necessary
If the *post facto* analysis is to have any merit, in fact, if the whole idea is to have any teaching value, then it is essential that the groups be given another problem as soon as possible after the analysis in order that they can implement what they have learned about effective group dialogue and problem solving.

The following is offered as a possibility.

The Gold-Rush Miners

During the days of the Cariboo gold rush, would-be miners like R. Byron Johnson had a lot of time on their hands, waiting for transportation to the gold fields. To keep busy, they would take up activities like foot-racing and weight-lifting. Others would try less exhausting sports like horseshoe pitching or even checkers.

Johnson found that he and his three best friends in the Cariboo each enjoyed a different one of the four activities. He was also impressed by the fact that he and each of his three friends had very different hair styles.

The problem is to figure out the names of R. Byron Johnson's three friends, to determine what activity each of the four miners preferred, and what hair style was worn by each of the four of them.

This is the additional information given to each student:

#1 Two of the miners had long hair, but one of them wore it in a braid because it kept his hair out of the way when he was engaged in his favourite sport. The other had shoulder-length hair worn loosely. Because this man was a weight-lifter, he did not mind hair falling in his eyes.

#2 At a horseshoe pitching tournament, Ramsay gave up his seat in the bleachers to an older lady and moved to the very back row. This was all to the good, however, since it meant he could sit beside Sawchuk. Ramsay and Sawchuk had made a bet on who was going to win the tournament and they wanted to watch the play together.

#3 Sawchuk was very fond of checkers. One day, when he saw Jacobs standing at the edge of a crowd of people in the street, he tried to talk Jacobs into a game. But Jacobs wanted to watch the weight-lifters competing with one another and told Sawchuk to find someone else.

#4 Because Johnson was rather short, he could barely see his friend at the starting line of a foot race one day. However, through a gap in the crowd he was able to see that the third racer from the left, bent over at the starting line, had short, straight hair, parted in the middle. Johnson knew then, for sure, that his friend was in the race.

#5 Since Jacobs' hair was rather short, he did not wear it in a braid. Yet, Jacobs always had trouble keeping his hair in place and he was secretly jealous of Johnson whose short, very curly hair was never mussed.

Suggestion Six: Maintaining the Momentum

Once the group discussion process is firmly established in a class of adolescents with learning problems, its use in the regular curriculum becomes a very straightforward procedure. However, there are certain factors a teacher should always keep in mind. These, basically, are the factors that make the "ODDO" problem or the "Miners" problem successful: namely, a clear purpose and direction for the group—they must know what is expected of them, and there must be a specific structure, organized by the teacher. Obviously, it will not always be possible in specific subject areas to generate group problems that lead to precise answers, as in ODDO or Miners. A group discussion of "causes" in a history class, for example, or a discussion of the impact of the setting in a short story, or a discussion in a science class of the effects of a specific environmental change, will naturally be much more open ended. Yet, a significant portion of the value of such a discussion is in the very dialogue itself: students talking naturally to and with one another on a topic of common concern.

Even at that, it is still possible for the teacher to ensure that the purpose of the group discussion remains clear by structuring the task for a specific outcome. (e.g. "Of the causes of the War of 1812 that your group determines, which one does the group feel is still unresolved today?" or "Would this story have ended as it did, if the setting had been different?") Also, it is almost always useful to have each member of the group, at the conclusion of the discussion, make notes for himself of what was discussed. Or if the teacher deems it beneficial—and it often is—the conclusions of each group can be collated in a teacher-directed lesson, preferably via a chalkboard note. The point is to make the group discussions concrete, to show that the effort of the discussions has a specific and culminating purpose. Without such concluding activity, the entire exercise will inevitably fall victim to the sense of purposeless gloom that pervades so much of the outlook of adolescents with learning problems. On the other hand, if there is a sense of achievement and purpose, then the momentum will continue.

A Final Thought

Since this chapter began with Scotty St. C., it seems appropriate that he should complete it. These, as faithfully as I can render them, are his own words.

> *"There were four of us new to the staff, that first year, and all of us tried the group discussion method. Only two of us still use it extensively. Because we each had "problem" classes, we were looking for a panacea—like all teachers with problem classes, I suppose. But there are no panaceas. The group discussion method is a fabulous technique, but it's only as good as the teacher who uses it. If you don't organize it carefully, and teach how groups work, and always make the goals clear to the kids, then they'll soon retreat from it. And you've got to be judicious too. You can't do group discussion all the time.*
>
> *But there's another important point:—one of us who dropped the technique was always worried that her students*

would miss something. She taught geography and was very strong about her subject. Yet, it's funny. I took geography for four years in high school. We didn't have one single group discussion, just standard lessons, and I don't think I remember a thing from them either! But then you don't have group discussions so kids will remember things. You have them so they'll learn to talk to and with other people. If kids with learning problems can learn to use oral language effectively, they have a better chance in life."

Bibliography

This chapter contains references to these titles.

Abrahams, R.D. and Troike, R.C. (Editors), *Language and Cultural Diversity in American Education.* Englewood Cliffs, N.J.: Prentice-Hall, 1972.

Bernstein, B., *Class Codes and Control.* London: Routledge and Kegan Paul, 1977.

Lawton, D., *Social Class, Language and Education.* London: Routledge and Kegan Paul, 1968.

Lawton,D., *Class, Culture and the Curriculum.* London: Routledge and Kegan Paul, 1978.

Vygotsky, L.S., *Thought and Language.* Cambridge, Mass.: MIT Press, 1962.

CHAPTER 8
TEACHING EFFICIENT THINKING STRATEGIES

MOST ADULTS approach the following activity in a fairly similar fashion. That is, they tend to use similar thinking strategies, as well as a similar sequence of strategies.

> *The idea of the activity is to enter the twenty-six letters of the alphabet into the twenty-six empty boxes. By entering the letters correctly, it is possible to make twenty-six words, each having something to do with the subject of MOVEMENT. For example, entering the letter R in the very first empty box produces the word MARCH.*
>
> *The letter entered in each box may be at the beginning of a word, or at the end, or in the middle. There are extra letters in each row which do not form part of the word; they are there simply to fill up the row (and to add to the challenge).*
>
> *No letters may be rearranged. A letter of the alphabet may be entered only once.*

Before reading further, try to complete the activity. It is on the next page.

The majority of adults, especially those who will read a book like this, generally adopt the following sequence of strategies. Initially, they rely on intuition, usually with fairly good results. By guessing, by calling upon their developed vocabularies and their general knowledge, they usually find RIDE in the second row, CHASED in the third, and while the fourth may slow them down, it does not take long for CREEP in the fifth. PASS is usually easy, but TROT and SWING in the seventh and eighth rows will slow some of them briefly. And so it goes. The typical adult, without any system or plan, will count on spontaneous, intuitive insights to provide most of the answers until about sixteen or seventeen, maybe even more, letters are entered.

At this point, that same adult will usually resort to a more deliberate strategy. She probably will, by reasoning and deduction, set out to determine which letters of the alphabet are as yet unused. (Extensive trials with this activity show that PACE, row 14, JUMP, row 16,

I	E	J	M	A		C	H	A	Q
T	X	F	R	I		E	G	K	P
O	M	L	G	C		A	S	E	D
R	L	O	H	I		E	U	D	I
U	V	H	F	B		R	E	E	P
O	Y	R	P	A		S	Q	M	O
I	P	T	R	O		M	J	R	Q
M	Z	P	K	S		I	N	G	N
R	S	M	V	B		L	I	D	E
W	G	A	L	L		P	B	A	L
N	X	U	Q	R		C	E	O	F
C	M	C	J	L		O	O	M	N
B	W	N	A	S		R	I	N	T
D	T	P	A	C		K	D	E	Q
J	N	F	S	T		R	K	X	R
G	S	Z	H	B		U	M	P	L
H	F	T	G	P		S	H	F	P
W	X	D	R	I		E	V	P	A
V	V	D	C	C		C	L	E	U
Z	N	L	W	A		K	H	K	N
A	I	P	B	S		U	A	K	E
S	X	T	U	R		Q	A	P	S
E	U	Q	V	E		P	A	N	D
O	T	D	R	I		T	C	J	T
V	C	L	I	M		P	G	R	U
Y	K	T	R	A		P	D	N	I

CYCLE, row 19, TURN, row 22 and DRIFT, row 24, cause the most difficulty.) Then, by a strategy of systematic exploration, she will attempt to insert each of these letters in an empty box until the correct one is obvious. Usually, this will complete the activity, provided all the letters, previously entered intuitively, are correct. If there is evidence of an error or if it is clear that one of the left-over letters will not "fit", the typical adult will then retrace her steps, using systematic exploratory behaviour for words which may have been completed previously, but about which she may have been uncertain. Almost always, this strategy will complete the activity correctly.

A small percentage of adults will begin the activity more cautiously, using a systematic exploratory strategy much earlier. While this procedure is much slower, it is, by the same token, less prone to error. In activities where the content is more difficult or the topic more abstruse than "Movement", a systematic exploration strategy may indeed be necessary right from the beginning. The point is that most adults have this strategy in their cognitive repertoire; most of them recognize when it is needed; and most of them, when it is necessary, will put it to use.

Adolescents with Learning Problems Think Differently

Here is where adolescents with learning problems usually differ. Many of them do not have such a strategy at ready command and, if they do, they tend not to use it. Some of them may sense the wisdom of employing some kind of systematic strategy but are uncertain about just what to do. Still others may have an undeveloped idea of how to proceed but, because they lack confidence in themselves, either fail to persist or make only a tentative and, usually, unsuccessful effort.

When faced with an activity like this, these adolescents usually begin like most adults: they will use a spontaneous, intuitive strategy. But because they have less knowledge and a smaller vocabulary to draw on, they are usually less successful. Inevitably, they begin to slow down. Some will begin to make random guesses; others will begin to react negatively. Most of them, ultimately, will simply stop with the activity incomplete. Without a strategy to draw on, without an alternative to turn to, simply giving up seems to be a normal response. Fortunately, there is not much harm caused when an adolescent retreats from problems like these word activities. But there is great harm when they give up on their required schoolwork. And, more often than not, their reason for giving up in both spheres is similar: they do not have strategies—efficient thinking skills—to turn to.

Of all the things that are supposedly "wrong" with adolescents who have learning difficulties, the one factor that seems to be common to all of them—a truth that is depressingly obvious to classroom teachers—is that these students do not think efficiently or effectively. Rather, they tend to be episodic, unspecific, and random in their thinking styles. They ignore vital information (especially instructions), give little credence to reason and deduction, almost never hypothesize or plan ahead, and, above all, are disorganized. Yet, they are as capable of learning and using efficient strategies as adults and their "normal" colleagues. They need only be *taught*—first, that there *are* strategies and, secondly, that they must *use* them. Herein, again, the teacher becomes the key.

Before and After: Learning Efficient Thinking Strategies

In a simple but revealing experiment using the activity on p. 96, twenty-two members of an "advanced" secondary school class were compared to twenty-two members of two "basic" classes. Both groups were given the activity without any preamble other than simple instructions. The results were interesting but not surprising. As one might expect and, as the following table demonstrates, the difference in the two groups was not small.

Systematic Exploration Pre-Teaching Activity

	N	Mean Age	No. Began Intuitively	No. Used Systematic Exploration	No. Completed in 20 min.	No. Gave Up in 20 min.	No. Completing Activity Correctly
Advanced	22	15.1	20	22	21	0	20
Basic	22	15.9	22	7	14	8	6

Even though two thirds of the basic students saw the problem through to the end, less than half of those who completed it did it correctly. Their results compared very unfavourably with those of the advanced group.

At this point, both groups were given some training in the use of systematic exploratory behaviour. The basic group was given extra attention. It was not only encouraged to use a systematic strategy but was also urged to control the data by writing down the alphabet and crossing out each letter as it was entered. One day later, both groups were given a post-teaching activity exactly the same in design, except that all the words were about MUSIC. Here is the activity they were given. Following it are the comparison results from the two groups.

L	F	J	A		O	R	N	H	C	I
E	B	A	N		R	M	B	G	T	U
O	K	A	J		Z	Z	D	L	W	T
U	G	F	T		B	A	J	M	O	I
M	X	C	P		A	N	O	E	F	X
W	B	B	U		L	E	A	O	Z	V
I	T	D	Z		H	O	I	R	T	S
X	H	S	I		G	K	G	L	Z	Y
S	A	V	L		T	R	U	M	D	K
C	O	N	C		R	T	B	J	T	W
V	K	H	D		H	I	S	T	L	E
L	M	S	A		O	P	H	O	N	E
U	J	L	U		L	A	B	Y	O	I
O	N	B	A		A	S	S	N	Y	C
W	N	L	R		U	A	R	T	E	T
T	N	P	I		E	R	D	H	U	K
L	R	H	U		B	A	W	Y	E	F
C	S	J	L		R	E	B	G	M	L
V	T	D	U		U	L	E	L	E	F
Z	X	X	O		G	A	N	V	K	G
Y	A	L	T		K	X	E	J	N	U
B	F	C	B		E	N	O	R	I	Z
V	K	T	I		I	T	H	E	R	O
L	S	J	G		I	O	L	I	N	Z
N	B	A	N		O	H	D	C	X	W
Y	E	F	I		E	B	N	G	S	M

Systematic Exploration Post-Teaching Activity

	N	Mean Age	No. Began Intuitively	No. Used Systematic Exploration	No. Completed in 20 min.	No. Gave Up in 20 min.	No. Completing Activity Correctly
Advanced	21	15.1	2	21	21	0	21
Basic	22	15.9	6	22	22	0	20

It is significant that the basic group made substantial gains over the pre-teaching performance—more than might be expected as a simple product of the "second-time-around" factor. What is especially significant—certainly to teachers—is that the basic group adopted and used a strategy they were taught. These students demonstrated that they are modifiable:[1] they *can* adapt and change; they *will* search for alternative strategies; they *can* think and they *can* learn efficient thinking strategies. What they need is someone to teach these strategies.

Before and After: Part Two

The same experiment carried on with two more activities which tapped a different kind of thinking strategy. Both activities produced similar results: in the pre-teaching activity, the basic group was diffuse, tentative, episodic, inattentive to detail, and unsystematic. But once they were taught a strategy and had practised it, they used it spontaneously to achieve a goal.

The first of the two activities is one which highlights a particularly frustrating cognitive inefficiency, typical of most adolescents: namely, their inattention to detail—the "Oh! I didn't see that!" phenomenon.

The activity is simple. One need only follow the specific instructions step by step. By the time the fifteenth instruction is completed, the words remaining will form a statement (reading down the columns).

Quotation Crossing

If you follow all the directions in order, you will cross out all the unnecessary words and will be able to read something that the Canadian statesman Thomas D'Arcy McGee said in 1865.

1. Cross out all the words ending in T in lines 2, 6, and 13.
2. Cross out all words beginning with F.
3. Cross out all two-letter words in Column D.
4. Everytime a word appears twice in the same line, cross out the first one.

[1]I owe the word—and a lot of advice—to Reuven Feuerstein. More on Dr. Feuerstein later.

5. Cross out all words with a K in columns C and E.
6. Cross out all words beginning and ending with the same letter.
7. Cross out all words with more than one B.
8. Cross out the third undeleted word in lines 4 and 8.
9. Cross out all words beginning with a vowel in lines 2 and 13.
10. Cross out all words ending in Y.
11. Cross out all words over two letters in lines 3 and 9.
12. Cross out all words with more than one M.
13. Cross out all words appearing twice in Columns A, B, and E.
14. Cross out all words with IE combinations and NG combinations.
15. Cross out all CH words in which the CH is pronounced "K".

	A	B	C	D	E
1	TIGHT	JOLT	ADVISORY	BABY	MOMENT
2	ASTER	MELT	FIEF	ILLEGAL	SENDS
3	BOMBAST	RAGE	AIR	TO	GAS
4	AND	FROM	IN	AND	STILL
5	HALF	EXPERIENCE	SING	OF	PULLEY
6	ENVY	WE	SNACK	WRIST	PROBABLE
7	GAG	MURMUR	DEAD	FASCINATE	LONG
8	FILL	ARE	THE	CALENDAR	TUCK
9	WIT	GO	ZEPHYR	IS	GO
10	FUNNY	JOLT	SAYS	WIENER	GLIMMER
11	CHORUS	BIB	CHEMICAL	MUST	KNOW
12	ON	FLUSTER	VALLEY	LUNGE	ON
13	PHOTOSTAT	ORANGE	CHLORINE	UNDER	MEAT
14	HALF	LOLL	RAPIDS	FLOOD	MUMBLE
15	MINIMAL	WIELD	BUBBLE	AT	LEERY

The results, for the advanced and basic groups on this pre-teaching activity, were as follows:

Attending to Detail Pre-Teaching Activity

	N	Mean Age	No. Completed in 30 min.	No. Gave Up in 30 min.	No. Completing Activity Correctly	No. with 2-4 Errors at Completion	No. with 5 or more Errors at Completion
Advanced	22	15.1	22	0	18	3	1
Basic	20	15.8	19	1	8	7	4

As with the activity involving systematic exploration, the basic group performed less ably than the advanced on this pre-teaching activity. (In the basic group, however, the number who persisted in the activity, despite a lack of initial success, was encouraging; probably an indication of their enjoyment of the work—something for teachers to build on.)

Following the completion of the first "Quotation Crossing", both groups were given instruction and practice in the simple but important matter of attending to detail. Emphasis was placed on the methodical, sequential processing of information and on the careful control of data by reducing and cross-checking. Here is the post-teaching activity they were given, followed by the results.

Quotation Crossing

There is a sentence hidden among other words in the diagram below. If you follow all the directions in order, you will cross out all the unnecessary words and will be able to read something that Sir William Van Horne, builder of the Canadian Pacific Railway, is reported to have said in 1920.

1. Each time a word appears twice in the same line, cross out the second one.
2. Cross out all words beginning with O.
3. Cross out all words of colour.
4. Cross out the five-letter words in lines 2, 7, and 14.
5. Cross out all words with double letters in Columns A and C.
6. Cross out all words ending in E in Columns B and E.
7. Each time a word appears twice in the same column, cross out the first one.
8. Cross out all compound words.
9. Cross out all words beginning with CH.
10. Cross out all words with more than one A.
11. Cross out all two H letter words in Columns A and D.
12. Cross out the second undeleted word in lines 3, 9, and 14.
13. Cross out all words with three vowels.
14. Cross out all animal words.
15. Cross out all words with double letters.

	A	B	C	D	E
1	NEWSPAPER	ABROAD	BLUE	BUT	AN
2	HAPPY	PAPER	NOT	HIGHCHAIR	TRAYS
3	PINK	COW	CHASE	DUST	CHUM
4	IT	PETTY	BALL	GAME	DONKEY
5	CHIRP	VIOLET	ANYONE	BUT	BUT
6	ODD	CORRIDOR	ODD	HOUSE	AMAZING
7	BEAVER	CANADA	FLAME	FOGBOUND	PILOT
8	PAJAMAS	BOGGLE	A	ORGANIZE	CHUM
9	LADDER	GOAT	SHIRT	BOILED	OPEN
10	SURPRISE	CHAT	A	HAZARD	FIRE
11	GEESE	LOBE	DAMAGE	LOBE	MUDDY
12	OTTER	TOOL	CHASE	IN	EDUCATION
13	DELETE	POKER	OLD	MINISTER	POKER
14	MISTY	LATTER	GLOW	FLOAT	LIGHTBULB
15	AT	IS	PUDDLE	SCARLET	IS

Attending to Detail Post-Teaching Activity

	N	Mean Age	No. Completed in 30 min.	No. Gave Up in 30 min.	No. Completing Activity Correctly	No. with 2-4 Errors at Completion	No. with 5 or more Errors at Completion
Advanced	22	15.1	22	0	20	2	0
Basic	20	15.8	20	0	19	1	0

Once again, the basic group demonstrated their modifiability. These results suggest that an inefficient cognitive style is *not* an absolute condition for adolescents with learning problems. This fact was underlined in the final portion of the experiment.

Before and After: Part Three

In the completing phase of the procedure, both groups were given pre-teaching and post-teaching activities of a more difficult nature. To solve them requires the strategy of establishing and testing hypotheses: the "if . . . then" approach so basic to efficient thinking. The pre-teaching activity is simpler than the post.

> *Recently, in a restaurant, I met three people who told me about the Liars Club whose members always lie, and the Truth Club whose members are absolutely committed to telling the truth. "Which club does each of you belong to?" I asked. X responded briefly but, as she spoke, a busboy dropped a tray of dishes and I did not hear what she said. Y spoke next. "X says she's a member of the Truth Club, and indeed she is. So am I." "Not so," Z interjected. "Y is a liars' clubber and I'm in the truth group."*
>
> *Who does belong to the Liars Club?*

Solving the activity requires establishing the straightforward hypothesis that X is either a Liars' Clubber or a Truth Clubber. If she is a member of the Liars Club, then she will report herself as belonging to the Truth Club. If she belongs to the Truth Club, then she will say so. Therefore, X's answer will be "Truth." If Y is a Liar, then he will say that X reported herself as a Liar. But he did not. Y quoted X as saying she was in the Truth Club. Since that is the only answer X could have given, Y must also be a Truth Clubber. Z, then, must be a liar.

Neither the advanced nor the basic groups found the problem very easy.

Establishing and Testing Hypotheses Pre-Teaching Activity

	N	Mean Age	No. Correct in 20 min.	No. Gave Up in 20 min.	No. Correct in 30 min.	No. Gave Up in 30 min.
Advanced	22	15.1	7	8	1	6
Basic	22	15.9	4	15	0	3

Extra time was taken for practice in this strategy since more students found it difficult. However, once they became accustomed to the process of posing an hypothesis and deducing consequences, students in both groups became quite proficient in the strategy. The post-teaching activity given them is quite difficult; yet, the results that follow are encouraging.

> *The tourist group you are leading becomes lost in a goldmine on the border between the countries of Kapeenia and Dafeelia. Eventually, you find your way out but you don't know which country you are in.*
>
> *Before you, stand a Kapeenian and a Dafeelian. Although they look exactly alike, you know that Kapeenians always lie and Dafeelians always tell the truth.*
>
> *What one question[1] can you ask them to find out where you are?*

Establishing and Testing Hypotheses Post-Teaching Activity

	N	Mean Age	No. Correct in 20 min.	No. Gave Up in 20 min.	No. Correct in 30 min.	No. Gave Up in 30 min.
Advanced	22	15.1	14	2	3	3
Basic	22	15.9	12	4	3	3

Once more, the gains posted by both groups showed that students can indeed learn and apply efficient processes—the processes necessary for productive and effective thinking. For teachers, the significance is in the fact that adolescents who have learning difficulties can learn strategies, that their thinking processes are modifiable.

Comparison with other Research

While no one would pretend that the consequences of this small experiment are earth-shaking, they are at least consistent with much of the limited research on the subject.

With the exception of Feuerstein's work (1979, 1980), most of the slim research has been concentrated on the negative end of things: generally establishing that adolescents with learning problems are poor thinkers. Havertape (1976), for example, found that they do not attend to

---

[1]The question is: "Is this your country?" If the answer from *either* of them is NO, then you are in Kapeenia; if YES, then you are in Dafeelia.

detail, that they miss relevant information, and respond impulsively and randomly. Impulsivity has been a particularly important topic of investigation, with most researchers demonstrating that adolescents who are having problems in school tend to rely on impulse over reason and intuition over organized behaviour (Hallahan *et al.*, 1970; Keogh, 1971; Messer, 1970; Wilcox, 1970). But the most important work in the field is probably that of Reuven Feuerstein. The brilliance of his achievements lies, first of all, in the fact that he has categorized and delineated the deficient cognitive functions typical of adolescents and others with learning problems, thereby giving teachers something concrete. But, also, in his wide ranging and extensive research and teaching, he has shown that these deficient functions can be curbed, that the learner can be modified, by teaching, to use efficient cognitive functions.[1] Feuerstein has confirmed what teachers know—that their non-achieving students do not think efficiently. But he has also confirmed what teachers have long believed but have found difficult to demonstrate—that efficient thinking can be taught.

The Thinking that Teachers Usually See

Teachers are all too aware that adolescents with learning problems don't, or won't, or, perhaps, even can't seem to think straight. With depressing regularity, teachers watch these students fail to employ the strategies that would help them be successful academically, or that would help them in social exchange, or that would be productive behaviourally.

Here, for example, is a brief log of events from one day early in the school year with one of my classes of "problem" adolescents. It is a catalogue of inefficient thinking that could have occurred in any such class. This one had been officially labelled the "opportunity" group.[2]

> *8:58 a.m.: Johnny K. jumped from his seat without permission and disappeared down the hall. He was seen and disciplined by the vice-principal for being out of his class during opening exercises. His explanation: he had just remembered something he wanted to tell his friend in another class (that the family cat had given birth!).*
>
> *9:10 a.m.: Six of the twenty-four in the class brought mathematics texts instead of atlases. Explanation: "Frank said it was Thursday!"*

---

[1]Feuerstein's teaching system is a non-verbal process called Instrumental Enrichment. The system that follows later in this chapter is built on Feuerstein's principles, but is verbal. The two systems are, in my opinion and in Dr. Feuerstein's, quite compatible.

[2]Sully (Chapter 4) once described placement in opportunity class as "throwing a drowning man *both* ends of the rope!"

10:03 a.m.: An exercise on intersecting latitudes and longitudes. Donna B. and Cassetta T. were on the wrong map. Explanation: "I thought you said Newfoundland" (Donna); "The one on this page is prettier!" (Cassetta).

10:51 a.m.: Guidance counsellor appears to request that Tino S., Horst P., and Jim V. be excused to rewrite an aptitude test. Explanation: It was a multiple choice test, and they had selected the first choice in every question.

10:52 a.m.: A discussion about the setting of a short story was halted in its tracks. The story was set on the New Brunswick coast. Because Zach R. had seen the words "cliff" and "rock-formation," he insisted that the setting was in the mountains. He was seconded by Ginny W. and Alton P. who began searching the text for other support. Meanwhile, Brian D. led a contingent who wanted to reject the story. Brian had been to New Brunswick and "there are no cliffs in New Brunswick nowhere!" A third group wanted to know why bother with setting anyway.

11:35 a.m.: Doreen K. stopped working and put her books away. Explanation: "I want to be ready for lunch." Lunch begins at 12:05.

1:45 p.m.: Tim B. returned from an orienteering field trip. He had been lost for the entire morning after he misread a diagram and turned left instead of right.

2:10 p.m.: Entire class missed a simple mathematics problem which posed that a triangle be formed by leaning a board against a wall. The top of the board was then to be moved down the wall, a distance of one metre, to form a triangle of a new shape and size. No one in the class reasoned that the bottom end of the board would have to move too.

3:10 p.m.: Dismissal occurred ten minutes ago. Besides the forgotten books, notes, pens, and papers, I picked up three umbrellas and a raincoat. It was raining heavily outside.

There were other incidents; these are only highlights. Nothing described above is new to a classroom teacher. Yet, the other side of the coin is always present and teachers know this as well. On that same day, Zach R. organized his own nomination to the slate of candidates for the student government. He was not elected but his campaign was clever. Tim B. and Lyle J. arranged an early dismissal system for the remainder of September because of the landscape maintenance contract they had set up with a senior citizen's home. Donna B. and her twin sister began the design of a bulletin board display for parents' night. Tim B. went back to his orienteering instructor with an explanation of why he had gone wrong and with a request for another try. In other words, while students like these show clear deficiencies in their thought processes, they also show ability and potential. Since they can learn to think efficiently, it behooves us, as their teachers, to attempt to show them how.

An Immodest Proposal: Teach Efficient Thinking

The remainder of this chapter describes a programme in cognitive development for adolescents with learning problems—a programme in teaching efficient thinking strategies. It is premised on a number of observations and assumptions that are the combined product of experience and common sense. The first of these is that this type of adolescent needs such teaching to show him that strategies like attending to detail are vital to his progress.

A second assumption is that the potential for developing sound thinking processes is present in all human beings, including adolescents with learning difficulties. It remains for teachers to awaken that potential, to help organize it, and to encourage its application in the widest possible manner.

A third is that maintenance learning—the acquisition of knowledge, of fixed outlooks, methods and rules for dealing with known and recurring situations—is simply not enough. It is important learning (hence the Skill Development and Subject Areas component in the SETSEM Model) but, by itself, maintenance learning is not sufficient. If it were, then drill and repetition alone would cure the problems of students who have learning difficulties. But taskbound training tends to have only its own effect. Sensitizing students to a process, however, like systematic exploration behaviour, helps them generalize to a wider world, not just the immediate world of school. Once students are taught sound thinking strategies, the maintenance learning in their school careers will have wider purpose.

A fourth issue grows from the very nature of this type of student. Any programme which attempts to teach efficient thinking skills to students with a history of failure must have as its primary vehicle material that is non-curricular-specific. Without question, a teacher of mathematics can find ample material for emphasizing the practice of *attending to detail.* An English teacher can find subject matter to teach the strategy of forward planning. Geography is a fertile area for *establishing and testing hypotheses.* All teachers of adolescents can deal with *reasoning and deducing,* with *divergent thinking,* with *identifying starting points,* no matter what their subject areas. But their audience is a wary one. To adolescents who know they have already failed in English, in mathematics, or geography, any new approach which uses the old familiar material in different clothing is bound to generate distrust, uncertainty and, likely, rejection. The teaching sequence in this programme is one which begins in neutral territory where efficient strategies are demonstrated with material they are not likely to have ever used. After success has been achieved, the student moves along to the standard curriculum and beyond it.

What are the Strategies to be Emphasized?

The following chart presents the strategies that have proven to be most important to this programme for adolescents with learning problems.

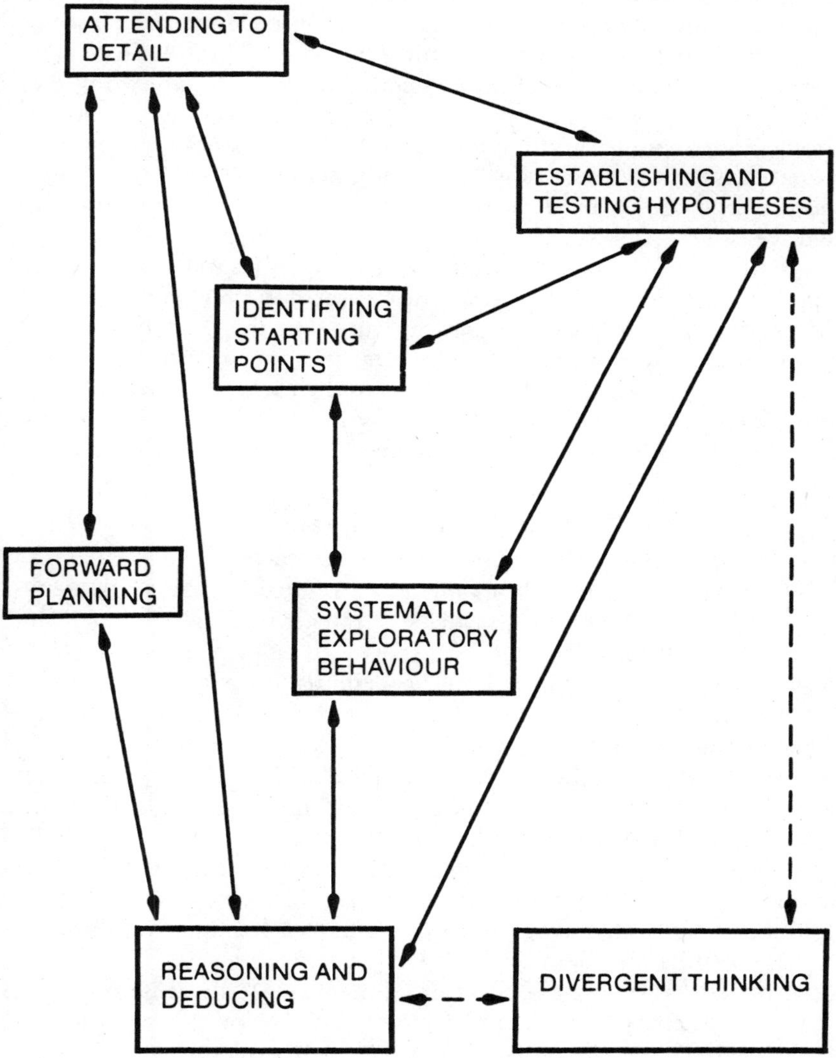

There are obvious caveats. No one would pretend that all the skills available to an effective thinker can be reduced to these seven. Nor can the seven be regarded as mutually exclusive—hence, the inter-connecting lines on the chart. However, these lines are really only symbolic as the possible connections are infinite.

Probably the strategies on this chart could be reduced to two: *divergent thinking* and *reasoning and deducing*. In these two, particularly the latter, the others are subsumed. Yet to do so would deny the reality of the way that adolescents with learning problems think. While divergent thinking as a total concept seems to be well within the potential competence of most of these students, reasoning and deducing seems to be too global a strategy for teaching purposes. There are too many essential components—such as *attending to detail, establishing and testing hypotheses, forward planning*, for the adolescent with learning problems to handle simultaneously. Experience—and experiment—shows that their potential for the development of efficient thinking is more easily tapped by approaching certain of these components in relative isolation until their use is firmly established.

Ultimately, the decision about which strategies to emphasize and when will be based on day-to-day observation of the students' thinking-skill needs. Only in the classroom can one make this determination. It was in the classroom that the seven strategies on this chart were first isolated for teaching purposes, and it is in the classroom that a teacher may choose to add to them, alter them, ignore some, expand on others. The decisions will depend upon the needs of the students.

Introducing the Programme

On the surface, this is one of those stages in the teaching process that is so self-evident that it hardly bears mention. Yet, teachers know that anything new presented to these students will meet with an automatic and immediate resistance born of wariness, weariness, and a perceived history of failure. This programme has certain advantages which, if they are utilized along with a careful introductory presentation, will overcome almost any initial resistance.

In the first place, the experience of innumerable classroom trials has shown that *all* students thoroughly enjoy the materials used in this programme. Secondly, to students resigned to words like "remedial", "compensatory", "modified", even the name: "a programme in the development of efficient thinking strategies" has appeal. Perhaps most important of all, this programme offers the teacher some responses to the litany of the Problem Student. For the answers to "Wadda we gotta do this for?" and "What good's this gonna do me?" are quite apparent.

Most teachers find that an effective opening move is simply to give the students an activity with no preamble other than the instructions.

The following activity is a straightforward one, and most students will succeed with it, if they attend to detail.

Ups and Downs

Jean is being followed into an office building by a very fast spy. In order to lose him, she gets into an elevator and presses several buttons. Starting at the first floor, she goes up 4 floors to the 5th floor:

then up 3 floors to the ______________ *floor;*

then down 4 floors to the ______________ *floor;*

then up 5 floors to the ______________ *floor;*

then down 6 floors to the ______________ *floor;*

then up 1 floor to the ______________ *floor.*

Now she gets off the elevator and runs up the stairs 2 floors. What floor is she going to?

After their students have had an opportunity to attempt the activity, the majority of teachers will verify the answer by solving it with them via the chalkboard or overhead transparency, being certain to be good models in attending to detail. As with all the activities in this programme, the *post facto* analysis is more important to the students than the activity itself. Hence, the teacher will probably dwell on factors that are useful in handling detail. (Why is it useful to make a diagram? Why is it useful to check off each piece of data as it is used? Why is it useful to re-check the data before deciding upon an answer?)

It is at this point, after the students have enjoyably and successfully completed an activity and after an analysis of why they succeeded,[1] that the majority of teachers will present the idea of a whole programme on efficient thinking strategies. Particular attention should be paid to how such strengths as attending to detail can be helpful in the students' lives inside and outside school.

Classroom trials have underlined the value of setting up the strategies chart (see p. 109) at this point in the introduction, as an attempt to whet the appetite and stimulate curiosity. The chart is presented to indicate the range of cognitive skills to be explored. The next step is simply to launch into the very first strategy. Usually, this will be attending to detail since students are already familiar with it.

---

[1]For those who are sensitive to the fact that a small minority may not succeed or to the reality that certain students will complete an activity more quickly than others, there are suggestions later in the chapter.

A Suggested Teaching Sequence for each Strategy

There is no intent here to prescribe either method or sequence in an absolute way, for prescription denies the joy of teaching. Here, nevertheless, is a procedure that has been successful over extensive trials and which is easily adaptable to the styles and preferences of individual teachers.

Step One:	Present the Strategy as a Concept.
Step Two:	Practice with Non-Curricular-Specific Activities.
Step Three:	Relate to Curriculum and to Wider Uses.
Step Four:	Reinforce (by periodic return to step two).

Step One: Presenting the Strategy

Experience indicates that the method suggested in the foregoing pages is very effective for introducing a strategy: namely, allow students to complete an activity which requires use of the strategy and then introduce the strategy *post facto* as a concept. Ideally, the activity presented at this step will be one at which the majority of students will certainly be successful. Only later in the programme, when students have grown in confidence, might it be advantageous to present an activity at which failure could be enlightening.

It is important to emphasize the conceptual nature of the strategy. Students should realize that forward planning, for example, is a process which has wide application. It is not simply something they use to complete an activity. It is a strategy; it is an idea; it is a life-skill. Teachers, therefore, may wish to reinforce this by creating an atmosphere in which the *idea* prevails. The classroom environment, for example, may stress the current strategy through signs and bulletin board displays. Brief daily discussions may seek out real examples of the strategy in use outside school. A guest speaker might be helpful: one of the teacher's acquaintances who would chat about the use of the strategy in his or her life. Whatever the method, it is essential that the students be aware that the process is not task-bound. Rather, it has wide and immediate application inside and outside school.

Step Two: Practice with Non-Curricular Specific Activities

Once the strategy has been introduced, the subsequent stage increases students' ease and familiarity with it, by practice. There is a basic principle here, instinctively well-known to most classroom teachers, but one which bears repetition. The primary objective of these non-curricular-specific activities is to develop the students' ability to use a strategy comfortably and effectively. Once this objective is achieved, there is not much point in continuing to use the activities, except as periodic reinforcers. The only purpose of Step Two is to reach Step Three.

Almost invariably, students find these activities enjoyable. Even the most jaded and bitter adolescents are caught up in the enthusiasm that becomes immediately apparent in a group. There is strength in this— and danger. The strength is that teaching is easier; adolescents who are resistant to almost every overture can be won over with this material. The danger is in the temptation to use the activities only because they are pleasing. The consequences of that practice are self-evident.

Step Three: Relate to Curriculum and to Wider Uses

In many ways, this stage is concurrent rather than sequential. Since the basic objective is to have students use each strategy in their school work and their life work, most teachers will blend this stage into Step Two as soon as possible. Then, as the students' competence in a strategy becomes apparent, Step Three will begin to dominate. This is the culminating point of the teaching procedure, the stage at which students employ a strategy in wider terms. Encouraging adolescents with learning difficulties to do so, however, will be a task left largely to the teacher. The teacher must lead the way in pointing out the utility of the various strategies in dealing with the regular curriculum. Just as teachers will monitor the procedure at Step Two until familiarity with the strategy is established, so will they lead and guide the application of the strategy at Step Three. Adolescents with learning problems are not likely to do so themselves; as always, they need their teachers.

Step Four: Reinforce

After a group of students has left Step Two well behind, it may be useful to return to a task-bound activity from time to time to emphasize a strategy. This may occur because a strategy is being ignored, or has fallen into disuse, or simply because the teachers decide that a review has become necessary.

Some Questions About Teaching Procedure

When I teach effective thinking strategies, do I concentrate on these exclusively? Not unless it is absolutely necessary to get the point across and, then, only at the very beginning. Remember, there is always a danger that students will develop the conviction that their programme in efficient thinking strategies is another subject, like mathematics or science, and it is not. The whole purpose of the programme is to teach processes that will be utilized elsewhere. Therefore, the sooner a teacher can show the usefulness of a strategy in the regular curriculum, the better.

Then what type of time frame should I expect to follow? An hour a day is sufficient, but the activities need not be presented every day. Once the introduction of the entire programme has been established, a teaching sequence of the following design has proven to be the most effective.

Monday: non-curricular specific activity plus follow-up discussion of the strategy needed to complete it

Tuesday: repeat of previous pattern with another activity

Wednesday: repeat of previous pattern but with a shorter activity, so that time will remain for a brief foray into the regular curriculum in a manner that will use the strategy

Thursday and Friday: regular curriculum, but with emphasis on the strategy and its use in that curriculum; assign students a weekend task of observing and noting the need for the strategy in non-school situations

Monday: from the observations made on the weekend, prepare the longest list possible of practical applications of the strategy; present an activity, if time permits

Tuesday: conclude the activity and hold *post facto* discussion; return to regular curriculum

From this point, the degree to which the strategy is emphasized and the frequency with which non-curricular activities are presented will depend upon the teacher's perception of students' needs (Steps Three and Four). These decisions are reasonably straightforward, if one continues to see the objective of each strategy as a means of making students familiar and comfortable with a process that they will then use. Many teachers find it useful to reinforce with an activity at the rate of about once a week.

How long do we stay on a strategy before launching into the next one? Students seem to develop strength in a strategy over about a one-month time block. This will vary as a factor of the emphasis given it by their teachers. To extend the time period for more than a month, however, means that one runs the risk of over-extending students' interest.

Do I teach my whole group at once? What about those who work very quickly or very slowly? That some students work at a widely variant pace from others is a reality teachers have always had to face. Usually, the difference in speed needs to be accommodated only during Step Two when students are working independently at non-curricular-specific activities. At this point, an effective practice is to have several examples of the same type of activity. The student who finishes more quickly can begin working on a second exercise or even a third, if necessary, until the teacher makes the decision that teachers always make: when to conclude a process and move on to the next step.

Do students work independently? At Step Two, this is usually the most effective method—provided the teacher is "floating" as a ready resource or a monitor. However, it may be desirable, from time to time, for a teacher or a student to lead a simultaneous, whole-group attack on an activity.

I'm only one of seven teachers for my adolescent group. Who teaches thinking? Me? All of us? Some of us? Unless all teachers—or almost all—are involved, it is entirely possible that students will develop the impression that "thinking" is something they do only in Ms. X's class. Despite this, there will be transfer of the strategy into other classes, even if it is never mentioned there. It is much more effective to have all teachers involved. The ideal process is to have one or two teachers function as principal instructors who introduce the strategy and utilize the activities in Step Two. All teachers then emphasize the use of the strategy in their respective subjects so that students see its wider application. There must be at least a minimal team effort among all teachers, if students are to realize the full benefits of learning efficient thinking strategies. Fortunately, most teachers of adolescents with learning problems realize that, without some kind of co-ordinated team process, much of their efforts are dissipated by confusion and contradiction. Co-ordination is essential.

Let's have some examples for a particular strategy. Okay. Let's look at attending to detail at each of the steps.

Attending to Detail

Step One

After the general idea of learning efficient strategies has been introduced, it is wise to move directly to a specific strategy. Announce the strategy about to be practised and focus on it by means of a poster or symbol. The students are then presented with a non-curricular-specific activity or several in sequence. The value lies in what the teacher does after the activity is complete: i.e., "What has been learned?" "Let's apply this learning to a similar activity."

Step Two

As every teacher knows, the first activity should be fairly easy. Since attention to detail is the skill being emphasized, there should be as few intervening elements as possible. "Quotation Crossings", such as those seen earlier in the chapter, are ideal for this step.

When students have completed the activity, the teacher will lead a discussion that enumerates the means by which students coped with all of the detail (e.g. proceeding in sequence, checking off steps as they were completed, attending to each word in a specific sequence so that no details were missed, re-checking upon completion).

After this analysis, students should immediately be given the opportunity to repeat the process with a similar activity to reinforce the points that were learned. Once that activity is completed and the teacher feels that further work on the same type of activity is unnecessary, the strategy can be applied to a different type of activity. The following activity requires attention to detail but, this time, the students must attend more carefully to sequence and do some simple calculation.

Bill is 5 years older than Lena, who is 3 years younger than Tom, who was born in 1935. They were all born on the same day—15 March.

1. *In what year was Lena born? (1935, 1938, 1940, 1945, 1932)*
2. *In what year was Bill born? (1932, 1936, 1948, 1933, 1940)*
3. *How old will Bill be in 1955? (25, 23, 22, 33, 27)*
4. *If they have an elder brother Harry who is 7 years older than Tom, how much older is he than Lena? (4, 5, 6, 7, 8, 10 years)*
5. *In what year was Harry born? (1932, 1930, 1924, 1928, 1929)*
6. *What is the sum of the difference between Harry and Lena's birthdates and Bill and Tom's birthdates? (14, 13, 12, 11, 10).*

As students become more conversant with the idea of manipulating detail, the activities might become more complex. Here, for example, is a reasonable follow-up activity to "Bill, Lena, Tom". Note that, even though it appears to be more difficult, it is simply an activity which requires careful handling of detail.

Ten years after the beginning of the Seven Years War, which ended in 1763, Hezekiah Beame arrived in Newfoundland with his family. At the time they arrived, Hezekiah was exactly half as old as his sister Rachel had been two years before the Seven Years War began. Rachel had celebrated her eighteenth birthday while crossing the Atlantic. How old was Hezekiah when he came to Newfoundland?

The discussions that follow each activity will invariably illuminate some strategic element for students. Using diagrams and writing down details so that they can be more easily understood and manipulated become necessities in these problems. While these are techniques that adults take for granted, it is not automatic for adolescents who have learning difficulties. The activity that follows, for example, is very easy, if students write down the details as they proceed. Otherwise, it causes confusion because of the overload of information.

Read the following carefully; then put the people A, B, C, D, E, and F in the order of their weight with the heaviest on the top:

A, B, and D are together heavier than A, B, and E.

A, D, and E are together lighter than A, F, and E.

D, E, and F are together lighter than D, E, and C.

A and B are together lighter than A and E.

A is heavier than B, but lighter than E.

It may be worth a slight digression to acknowledge that many of these problems appear strikingly simple, especially to the kind of adults who will read a book like this. Further, it seems obvious that, in dealing with chunks of detail and data, one must obviously record information, organize it in sequence, and then act on it. Yet, as teachers of adolescents with learning problems will quickly agree, this is something their students do not do, either automatically or on instruction. They have to learn, through experience, the efficacy of such a procedure. Students must realize the value of attending to detail and learn also how to cope with it. By discovering that they can handle masses of information, they necessarily become less intimidated by it. They find greater success, therefore, with the regular curriculum and also develop an extremely important life skill.

Step Three

At this transition stage, the role of the teacher is paramount. Students will take their cues from teachers in the extent to which they apply, practically and automatically, the strategy they are learning. If each teacher stresses the use of the strategy in her subject, then her students are far more likely to make the transfer from task-bound demonstration activities to wider applications.

A teacher of mathematics, therefore, might present a problem with a view to having his students list both the details to be covered and the sequential steps before attempting the problem. A teacher of English might emphasize the strategy by assigning a passage to be read for the specific details which support a premise made by the author. Geography lends itself admirably to demonstrating the significance of attending to detail, as do history and science. It is vital that students develop the habit of using the strategy automatically, that they learn to include it in their repertoire of techniques for dealing with their world. Teachers, by example and by teaching design, can help students arrive at this state.

Step Four

A periodic return to non-curricular-specific examples of a strategy serves as a reminder to students of the value of a strategy. It is also one of the means by which a teacher attempts to develop the automatic use of a strategy by students. It may also be advisable to use an activity to bolster the outlook of students whose confidence in a strategy is flagging or even to challenge those who may begin to think it is superfluous. In the former case, an activity like "Famous Countries" will serve because of its simplicity. In the latter, one like "The Basketball Game" is useful.

Famous Countries

By following the instructions, you will discover the names of two famous countries. Read all the instructions first.

Step 1: The first letter is the eighth letter from the end of the alphabet.
2: The next letter is two letters before E.
3. The next letter is one letter after N.
4. The next letter is in the number twenty position in the alphabet.
5. The next letter is in the number twelve position in the alphabet.
6. The next letter is two before C.
7. The next letter is between M and O.
8. The next letter is directly above Q.
9. The next letter is three before F.
10. The next letter is before B.
11. The next letter is four letters before R.
12. The next letter is directly above N.
13. The next letter comes after C but before E.
14. The last letter is the first letter of the alphabet.
15. The problem is easy if you first write out the alphabet in two rows, A to M and then N to Z directly underneath.

The Basketball Game

A basketball game is being played between teams A (odd numbers) and B (even numbers). There are 4 periods, each 15 minutes long. A basket is worth 2 points and a foul shot is worth 1 point. From the information given, find each player's score as well as the team's total. Which team wins? Is the score 126-122? 132-130? 130-126? 135-124? 128-120? 130-120?

Player #35 scores 3 points every 4 minutes but she is injured and taken out with 5 minutes left in the third period.

Player #38 has 72 shots for baskets and is successful 1/3 of the time.

Player #20 plays only the first half. She shoots for baskets every 3 minutes and is successful 50% of the time. She has 4 foul shots and is successful 1/4 of the time.

Player #29 scores 1 basket every 6 minutes. She has 6 foul shots and is successful on 50%. She leaves the game with 6 minutes left.

Player #8 has a total of 52 shots. She scores a basket 25% of the time.

Player #23 scores 1 foul shot every 1.5 minutes for the whole game.

Player #3 has 12 foul shots and is successful 75% of the time.

Player #10 scores 1/6 as many points as Player #38.

Player #13 has a total of 50 shots for baskets and scores a basket 10% of the time.

Player #17 scores 1/5 the number of points that #13 does.

Player #18 scores a basket every 5 minutes. She has 12 foul shots and is successful 33-1/3% of the time.

Player #6 replaces Player #20. She has 9 foul shots. Her percentage of success with foul shots is triple that of Player #18.

Player #7 always scores a basket once every five minutes. In this game she replaces Player #35.

Reinforcement of a strategy should take place over an extended period and, ideally, will never stop. However, as new strategies are introduced, the rate at which previously learned ones are reinforced will necessarily decline. The rate, the frequency, and the choice of activity are, as always, at the discretion of the teacher.

Are all the strategies covered in the same way? With the exception of divergent thinking, all the strategies are taught in a process basically similar to that described on the previous pages. What follows are examples of non-curricular-specific tasks in the remaining strategies and a brief discussion of each strategy.

Systematic Exploratory Behaviour

The ability to approach a task systematically and in an organized fashion is essential to much of problem-solving, to data gathering, and to various levels of analysis. For adolescents with learning problems, the strategy offers an even more fundamental benefit in that it gives them a technique for *getting started.* So frequently their avoidance of schoolwork is a product, not of being unable to perform, but of being unable to begin. Very often, they do not know where to begin or how to begin. With the strategy of systematic exploratory behaviour in their cognitive repertoire, they have a method of attack to which they can turn.

Sample Activities

The few examples here are sufficient to demonstrate the idea that systematic exploratory behaviour is a *process*: a process by which one arbitrarily selects a beginning point and then follows a logical sequence until an appropriate answer is logically determined.

In "Number Fill", for example, it makes sense to systematically and sequentially insert the available numbers below the graph until the correct mathematical statements are achieved.

In a sense, systematic exploratory behaviour is a rationalization of trial and error. The latter is a technique that these adolescents indeed use but, because they use it episodically and randomly, it is frequently unsuccessful.

Number Fill

Below each graph is a set of numbers. By filling the empty squares with these numbers and by following the arithmetic signs, you can arrive at the figures given in the bottom row AND in the right-hand column. You may use only the numbers below the graph and only as many times as they are given.

Y

3 3 4 4 5 6 7 8

Z

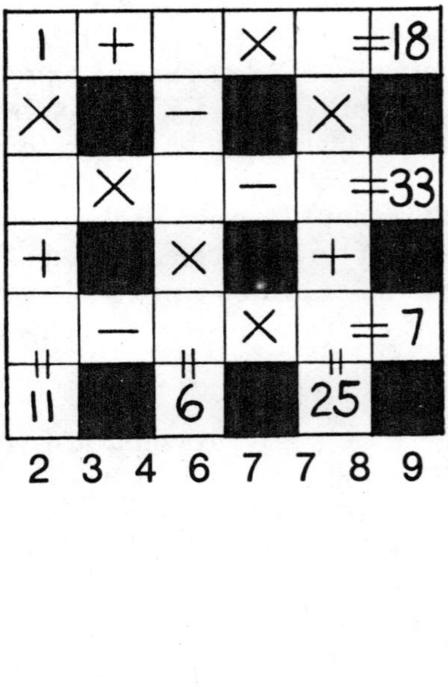

2 3 4 6 7 7 8 9

Although this next activity appears difficult, it submits nicely to a systematic exploratory approach. A solution is much more easily achieved, if one records all attempts. This practice of recording attempts is essential to any problem that requires an exploratory approach.

Set ten sticks in a row.

In as few moves as possible, arrange the sticks in a row of five crossed sticks.

You can move only in jumps and you must jump over two sticks in each move. A pair of crossed sticks counts as two. You can jump either left or right. It is possible to accomplish this in five moves.

The fact that systematic exploratory behaviour is a specifically sequential strategy does not imply that it is so lock-step as to preclude divergent thinking. Each of the two activities that follow yield to a systematic exploration of the relationships among the numbers, but one must first try to discover how many varieties of relationships there are to explore.

What are "a" and "b"?

5	11	8
8	14	11
a	26	23
12	18	15
36	b	39

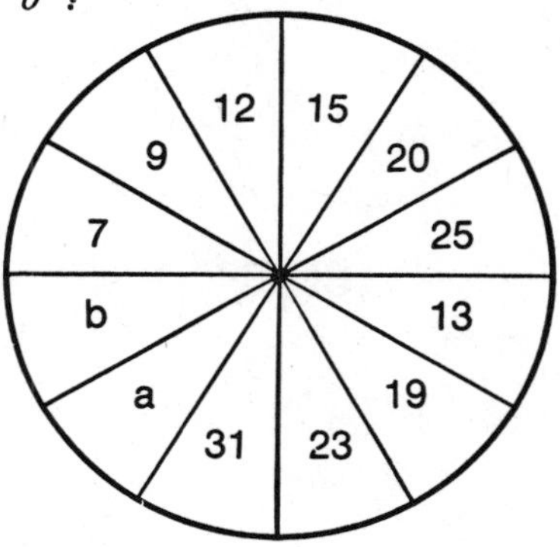

These are a few of the types of activities a teacher might use to teach the strategy. Even the ever-popular and widely available "word search" puzzles can prove valuable, if they are used to demonstrate the efficacy of a systematic approach. Any activity, if it helps to make the use of the strategy automatic in an adolescent with learning problems, can be worth the time and effort.

Establishing and Testing Hypotheses

Certain strategies like this one tend to pose more initial difficulty for all students. It is often advisable, therefore, to begin Step Two activities with teacher-led sessions. Under the guidance of someone who is reasonably confident in the process, students soon learn that the skill of hypothesizing—the strategy of assuming a piece of information and, therefore, determining necessary consequences—is not an impossible task. By and large, that is what establishing and testing hypotheses is all about: examining a problem to note what additional information would be helpful; hypothesizing the unavailable information; determining the consequences of the hypothesis: "if . . . then" thinking.

Sample Activities

An opening demonstration of this strategy can be made effectively by involving strategies previously learned (especially attending to detail and systematic exploratory behaviour since these two spread into all thinking). The following problem, for example, is best solved by hypothesizing where any one of the players is sitting and then, by systematically exploring the remaining data and attending to details in sequence, one either rejects or confirms the hypothesis. A diagram is very helpful and, as usual, if the problem is to be solved systematically, it will be helpful to record attempts so that incorrect hypotheses can be discarded and not repeated.

> *Two women, Evelyn and Geraldine, and two men, Harold and Fred, were seated around a table arguing about which card game to play. One was a bridge player, another played canasta, a third preferred poker, and a fourth, cribbage.*
>
> *The player arguing for bridge sat on Evelyn's left.*
>
> *Geraldine and Harold sat next to each other.*
>
> *The canasta player sat across from Fred.*
>
> *A woman sat on the poker player's left.*
>
> *The table is square, and each player sits at one of the four sides.*
>
> *Who wants to play cribbage?*

The *post facto* analysis should always emphasize the effectiveness of the "if . . . then" approach, since adolescents who have demonstrated poor achievement in school do not generally seem to find hypothesizing a natural process. For example, in the previous problem, if Geraldine sits on Evelyn's left, then Harold must be opposite Evelyn, and Fred opposite Geraldine. Then Geraldine must be the bridge player, which is not possible since the canasta player is opposite Fred. The hypothesis must be discarded. Moving along systematically, if Harold sits on Evelyn's left, then . . .

An alternative beginning activity might be the following one. This task emphasizes the use of "if . . . then" with less data to control than in the card players' problem.

Divided Line Drawing

This is called a divided line drawing:

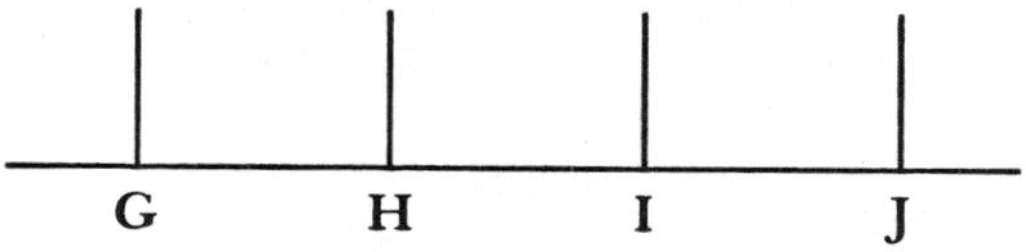

One can make true and untrue statements about this divided line drawing. For example, GHI, HIJ, GIJ, JIG, IHG are true statements whereas statements like HJI, GIH, JHI are untrue.

On the other hand, not HJI *and* not GIH *are true statements, whereas* not GHI *and* not GIJ *are untrue.*

Try the following questions.

1. In this divided line drawing —

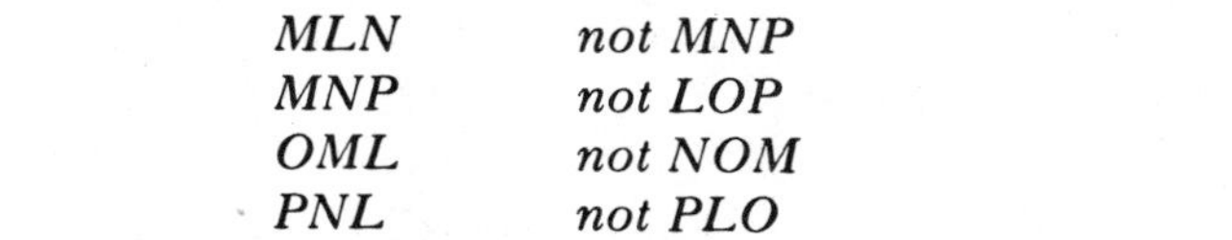

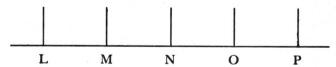

which of these are true statements?

ADC	*not OLM*
MLN	*not MNP*
MNP	*not LOP*
OML	*not NOM*
PNL	*not PLO*
PMN	*not LMP*

2. *Imagine that, for a certain divided line drawing, the statements STU and SRU are true; then which of the following statements* must *(without doubt) be true also.*

   SRT
   STR
   URS
   UTR
   none of the above

   If STU and SRU are true; then which of the following statements must, *without doubt, be true also.*

   not SUR
   not UTS
   RTS
   TUR

   Suppose not STU is true. Then which of the following must be true?

   not SUT
   not UTS
   SUT
   UTS
   none of the above

   If STU and TUR are true, then which of the following are not true?

   RST
   STR
   SUR
   UTS
   none of the above

   Suppose STU and USR are true; then which of the following is true?

   RTU
   SRT
   TSU
   URT
   none of the above

At this point students should be encouraged to generate their own hypotheses by preparing their own divided line drawings, with questions, to be practised by their classmates.

Sometimes the "if . . . then" approach can be encouraged by structuring an activity which poses the hypothesis for the students and then invites the determination of the consequences, as in this activity.

An ox-cart moves at a rate of 2 km per hour. Its' owner can walk at twice that speed. A train usually averages a speed at least 30 times that of an ox-cart. If a man has to travel from town to his home, would it be faster to go by train, half-way, and then by ox-cart, or to walk all the way?

Other problems might make the consequences obvious, but require the students to determine the appropriate hypotheses. In the following activity, for example, the consequences are fairly obvious.

Just before boarding the plane to fly to the tournament, golf pro John Peters receives this telegram.

"Of the eight approved golfballs you will use, one is sabotaged. It is one milligram heavier than each of the other seven. Do not use it."

The tournament rules permit a player to weigh approved golfballs on a balance scale only, and before a tournament each player is allowed only two weighs. How should Peters use the balance scale to identify the heavier ball?

When the heavier golf ball is placed on one side of the balance scale, that side will go down. The nub, however, is the establishing of the hypothesis: "If a certain number of balls are placed on each side of the scale . . ."

As students become more proficient, they can be given activities which require establishing a series of hypotheses in a particular sequence. The following activity is of that type. It also encourages attention to detail and the recording of data.

Sir Harold and Lady Bidigare were captured in the battle of Grosse Pointe Farm and imprisoned along with a servant in one of the highest towers of their castle. They escaped almost immediately, however, using equipment that masons had left while repairing the tower.

Just outside the window, a bracket stuck out from the wall. A rope with large empty baskets at each end hung over the bracket. The masons had used this equipment to haul stones up from the ground. By placing uneven weights in the baskets, the heavier would go down and the lighter would be brought up. The difference in weight was never greater than five kilos so that the heavier basket always went down slowly.

Use the following facts to explain step-by-step how Sir Harold and Lady Bidigare, with their servant, got to the ground safely, using the masons' method and equipment.

Sir Harold weighed 80 kilos
Lady Bidigare weighed 40 kilos
The servant weighed 45 kilos
Sir Harold's breastplate weighed 25 kilos
His chain mail weighed 10 kilos
His shield weighed 10 kilos
His helmet weighed 5 kilos
The servant was unconscious

Of the seven strategies suggested in this programme, establishing and testing hypotheses seems to require more practice and more careful leadership from the teacher than any other. This may be owing to the seemingly inherent reluctance of adolescents with learning problems to foresee or even consider consequences. In any case, once learned, the strategy is a useful and effective one and, if teachers encourage its use in Step Three, the results are worth the extra effort.

Identifying Starting Points

Avoidance behaviour in adolescents with learning problems frequently expresses itself as a factor of their not knowing where or how to find a way into a task. Classroom teachers are all too aware of that sensitive moment in a lesson when the students must begin to apply the principles of what has just been taught. This is the moment when the "I can't," "I won't," "What'm I supposed to do?" phenomenon strikes, largely because the students feel confused by data and do not know where to concentrate their initial efforts. This particular strategy, identifying starting points, is designed to show that knowing where to begin is a skill, and that examining a task for a beginning point is a strategy one must learn to use.

The activities in Step Two should teach students to make a careful examination of a task so that they will find its most logical starting point. The problem that follows contains data that, on the surface, are sufficiently convoluted to frighten off many people.

Mary Pat is seventeen years old. Her brother Stephen was born seven years after their brother Michael. Two years ago, Mary Pat was three times as old as Stephen. How old will Michael be when Stephen is as old as Mary Pat is now?

Yet in spite of the apparent complexity of the problem, a starting point is available in the third sentence. Once one realizes that two years ago Mary Pat was fifteen years old, Stephen then must have been five years old. Michael would have been twelve (from sentence two). From here, it is simply a matter of attending to the details and processing them in a logical sequence. The key is simply to examine the data for the starting point.

"Arithmetic circles" (following) are a useful practice task for this strategy. The idea is to insert the numbers 1 through 9 inclusive in the centre of each circle, using each number once. The sum of the numbers inserted into adjacent circles must then equal the numbers present in the overlaps. In the following task, for example, the number entered into the top circle, when added to the number entered in the circle on its adjacent left, must equal 5 and, when added to the number entered on its adjacent right, must equal 6.

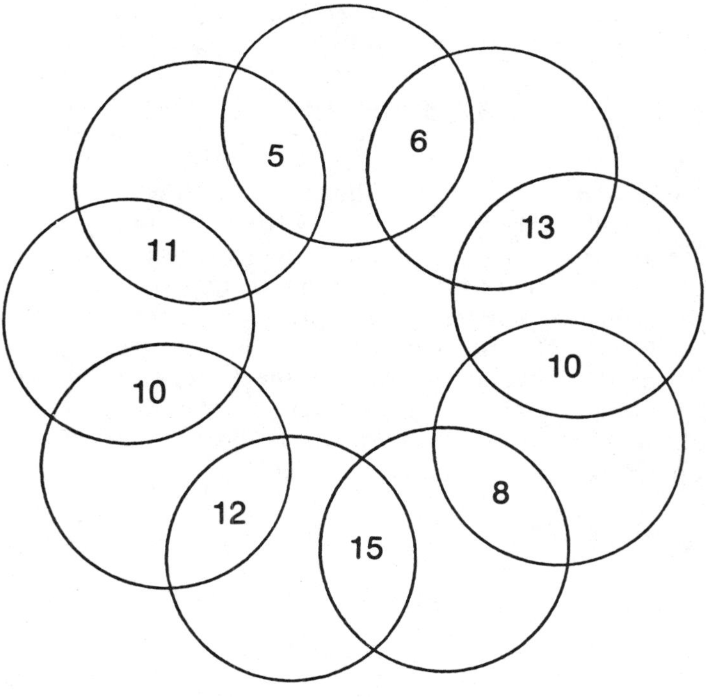

When a starting point is identified, a task like this yields easily to solution. The key is finding a starting point and, for this, students should look to the smallest or largest overlapped numbers. For example, in the circle next to 5, only the numbers 1 through 4 are possible. Therefore, by hypothesizing each of these numbers systematically, it does not take long to determine the correct one. The rest of the problem follows easily.

A similar situation obtains with an activity like this. It is a simple arithmetic problem, except that letters have been substituted for numbers. On the surface, such activities appear difficult to many students, principally because they do not know how to begin.

$$
\begin{array}{rcccc}
 & X & Y & Z \\
 & & Z & Y \\
+ & Z & X & Y \\
\hline
V & W & Y & Z
\end{array}
$$

In this addition activity, a starting point is in the right hand column; Y added to Y plus Z produces a number ending in Z. What number added to itself, plus a third number, will produce a sum ending in that third number? Systematic exploratory behaviour then shows that Y could only be 0 or 5. By testing each as an hypothesis, 0 is eliminated and Y, therefore, is 5. From this point, systematic hypothesizing will solve the problem.

A knowledge of very simple arithmetic will solve other such activities with equal ease. It requires only that one find a point to start.

Practice in this strategy also encourages students to utilize the practical habit of writing down information, thereby making it easier to manage. In the next activity, for example, students are asked to break a very simple code. These are famous cities of Europe; each figure stands for a letter. If students first write down the names of many European cities, they will note certain patterns: that many of them end in N for example. With this as a starting point, it is easier to hypothesize some of the more obvious choices, such as LONDON.

? ½ : % ½ :	% ″ $? ; :	X ½ ¼ = : 3 / Y = :
½ # ? ½	2 ½ @ =	@ / % 2 ; %
? ; # $ ½ :	$ = 2 ? ; :	$ = 2 : =
¼ / 2 ; #	/ ! 3 = : #	$ ½ : :

Like other strategies, identifying starting points is ultimately useful only if it becomes part of the students' automatic repertoires. Probably the most important aspect of this strategy is simply demonstrating to students that the tasks they face, even the thorniest ones, do have points at which to begin. For those students who are instinctively attuned to retreat, recognizing and acknowledging this fact is a major step forward. Acting upon this assumption as a matter of course is an even greater accomplishment.

Forward Planning

Generally, adolescents do not plan ahead. Of the many explanations offered for this phenomenon, none suggests a remedy. The following material is not a panacea for this particular ill. But it does offer this much: a means of demonstrating, harmlessly and with immediate results, the efficacy of forward planning. Students, after working with the non-curricular activities in this strategy, will at least be aware that thinking several steps ahead can be productive.

Step Two in this strategy seems to be most effectively covered in a competitive game format, such as the following one, "Spingo."

Players: *2 or more (preferably 4-5)*

Materials: *pencils and blank five-by-five grids*

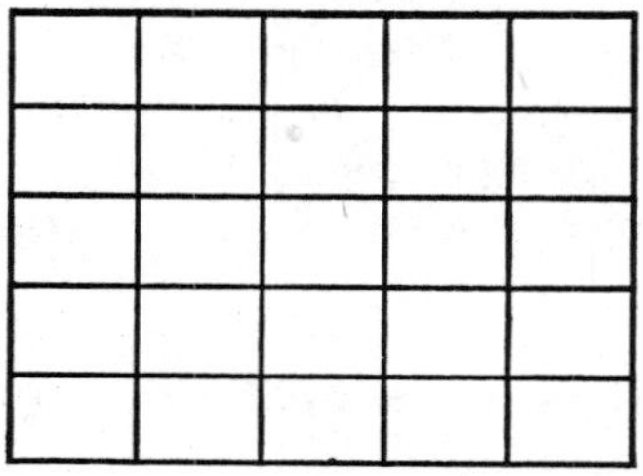

Play: *Players take turns calling out letters of the alphabet. Everyone, including the caller enters these letters into their grids as they are called, filling any squares they wish. The object is to make as many three-, four-, or five-letter words as possible by the time the grid is full.*

Scoring: *Three letter words in any straight row, column, or diagonal: one point.*

Four-letter words: three points.

Five-letter words: five points.

Overlaps count. For example, the word BOLD would generate three points as a four-letter word plus one point for OLD. Scoring is counted from both directions. For example, AET is worth one point (TEA), as is LOB from BOLD. However, a word counts in two directions only if it is lexically distinct in each case. For example, TOT would generate only one point because it is TOT in both directions. However, LIVE would earn three points plus three points for EVIL.

The benefits of planning ahead are self-evident in "Spingo." Even so, experience has demonstrated certain factors which impinge upon the pedagogy of the exercise. In the first place, students invariably plunge ahead without first considering whether proper names or slang are to be accepted. Here, for the teacher, is an initial demonstration of the need for forward planning. Secondly, students are usually more susceptible to the idea of forward planning after playing the game at least once. Once students are familiar with it, they can be encouraged to plan ahead if one or two new conditions are added each time they play. (e.g. a certain letter used in a word is worth bonus points; words with double letters are worth bonus points.)

Finally, the scoring process is a good test of the ability of students to process information systematically and sequentially. If students attend to detail in a systematic way, they are likely to record all the words and points they have earned. If they are episodic and random, words will inevitably be missed. Teachers can encourage systematic behaviour by suggesting that students exchange grids after their scores have been totalled. Anyone finding an unnoticed word in an opponent's grid is awarded those points.

The many benefits of forward planning strategy are self-evident. Yet, in a world where adults consistently fail to use the strategy, it is not surprising that adolescents with learning problems fail to do so as well. If students can be made to see the value of using the strategy and can also see that it is accessible to them, they will put it to use, especially if encouraged to do so by their teachers.

Here, for the discretionary use of teachers, is another game designed to promote forward planning.

OBJECT

The object of the game is to capture triangles. Some triangles are worth more than others. Certain combinations of triangles are worth more than others.

RULES OF PLAY

1. *The game may be played by 2 or 3 or 4 players.*
2. *Players take turns connecting any two dots, thereby forming the wall of a triangle.*
3. *The player who completes the third wall of a triangle, captures that area and gets a free turn. In this way, a player may capture several areas before someone else gets a turn.*
4. *A player who captures an area* must always *take a free turn.*
5. *Each player who captures an area should put an initial, or other symbol in that area.*

SCORING

1. *Each captured area is worth one point.*
2. *Players capturing any of the six cities get an additional five points per city.*
3. *Capital cities are worth an additional two points each.*

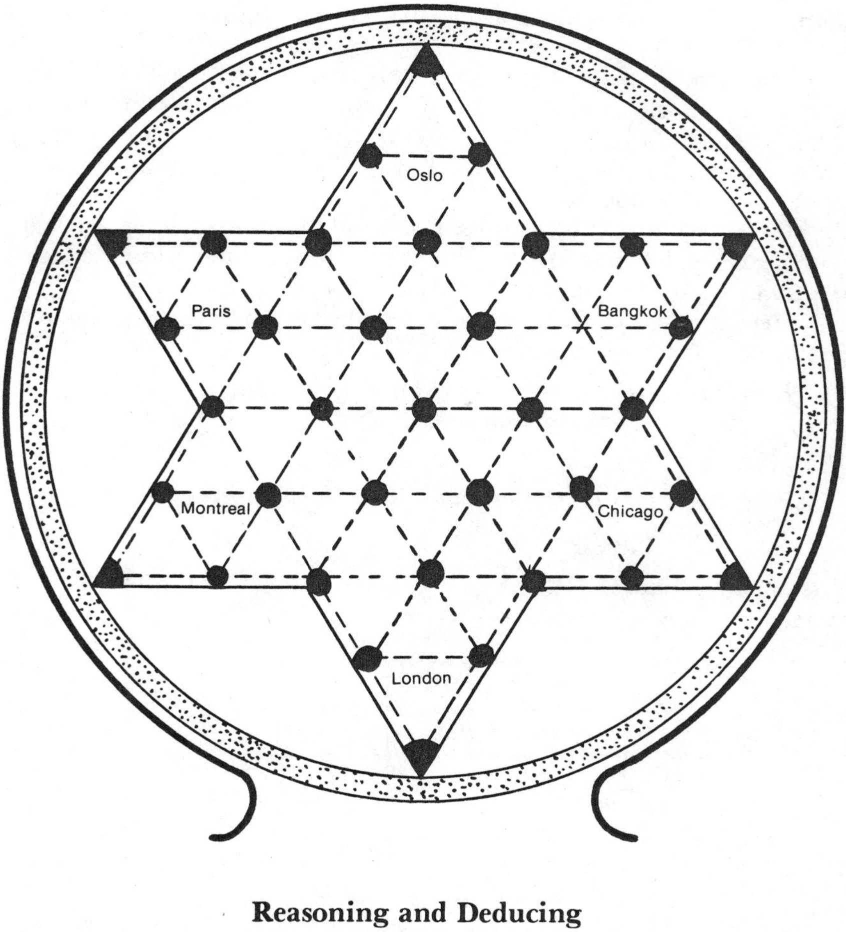

Reasoning and Deducing

In many ways, this strategy is a culminating one for the previous five. In the process of reasoning and deducing, one inevitably hypothesizes and plans ahead; it is necessary to explore systematically, to attend to detail, and to identify starting points. Yet, reasoning and deducing is more than the sum of all these. It uses them all but goes farther. In the process of reasoning and deducing, one must learn to manage the inter-relationships of pieces of information—to deal with chunks of data, the individual pieces of which are interdependent in a variety of ways. One learns the process of using two pieces of information to come up with a third, the process of organizing information so that it is of more use, the process of extrapolating, of making reasonable assumptions and reasonable conclusions. To teachers of adolescents with learning problems, the strategy of reasoning and deducing means to teach them a skill that will help them manage the mass of information that intimidates them into failure.

The basic objective at Step Two is to present students with activities that will first give them practice in organizing information into a manageable context and, then, give them practice in acting on that information so that from it they can extrapolate hitherto unknown facts, by reason and deduction. Because deductive problems are interesting, the students are usually well motivated and, if problems are presented with a gradual increase in difficulty, they will likely use all their capacities and develop the confidence to use this strategy with effect.

Here are a few examples of methodology in solving deductive problems. (Charts are always useful.)

Harold, Inez, Maria, and Rajit are 8, 10, 12, and 14 years old, but not necessarily in that order.

Maria is older than Rajit but younger than Harold.

Inez is younger than Maria but older than Rajit.

What is each person's age?

First, make a chart. It will be a two-way chart, since there are two factors to relate: names and ages.

	8	10	12	14
H				
I				
M				
R				

Then, use the clues—the available information—and enter these into the chart. (Please follow the entries below by alphabet letter.)

(a) Since Maria is older than Rajit she cannot be the youngest (8), and since she's younger than Harold she cannot be the oldest (14), so enter this information on the chart.

(b) Since Inez is younger than Maria, and Maria can only be 10 or 12, Inez must be 10 and Maria 12.

(c) Since both Inez and Maria are older than Rajit, he must be 8.

(d) This leaves Harold who must be 14.

Here is another example, a little more complicated.

> *Bette, Andre, Silvio, and Mai-Ling are in the annual school play, as a salesperson, a plainclothes detective, a technician, and a taxi driver.*
>
> *1. The director is very pleased with the way that Andre, Silvio, and the salesperson are doing their quarrel scene.*
>
> *2. Mai-Ling, Andre, and the technician are under surveillance in the first act.*
>
> *3. Everyone but the detective has a speaking part.*
>
> *Who plays what role?*

Again, it is wise to begin with a chart. There are only two relationships to discover, names and roles, so a two-way chart is all that is necessary.

	S	D	T	T-D
B				
A				
S				
M-L				

Notice how clues can be entered.

(a) From clue 1, neither Andre nor Silvio can be the salesperson, so enter (a) in those spaces.

(b) From clue 2, neither Mai-Ling nor Andre can be the technician and probably neither is the detective. Enter (b).

(c) It is now apparent that Andre is the taxi-driver, so enter a • there. If he is the taxi-driver, the others cannot be, so enter (c).

(d) This shows that only Mai-Ling can be the salesperson so enter a • there. Bette can't be the salesperson, so enter (d).

(e) From clue 3 and clue 1, we know that Silvio can't be the detective. Enter (e). So he must be the technician. Bette cannot be the technician (enter (e)), so she must be the detective!

Practise now on this one:

Dinah, Cathy, Luis, and Ned each have been given a lucky number in a lottery. The numbers are seven, four, two, and twelve.

One of the boys has the number two.

Cathy and the girl who has the number four are on the swimming team.

No one's name has the same number of letters as there are in his or her lucky number.

Or this one:

Four cars are parked in reserved spaces 21, 22, 23, and 24 at Acme Think Tank Company. The cars are grey, red, white, and yellow.

The yellow is not in 21.

The red is between the grey and the white.

The grey is between the yellow and the red.

Which car is in which spot?

Try this one, using the chart below.

In Room 7, there is a very small class of four students: two boys and two girls. Their last names are Lorge, Thorndike, Binet,

	TOM	*ANTOINE*	*EMELIA*	*YVETTE*
THORNDIKE	•		*(1)*	*(1)*
BINET		•	*(1)*	*(1)*
LORGE			•	*(3)*
WECHSLER				•

and Wechsler. Each is very good at different card games. One is a whiz at pinochle; another is a canasta expert; one is unbeatable at rummy; and the fourth is a champion double solitaire player. All of them, Tom and Antoine, Emelia and Yvette, get along very well together.

Find out each person's name and specialty.

1. *Thorndike, who does not play rummy thinks he is better at his game than the girls are at theirs. Binet believes he is better than the girls too, but is unwilling to play them.*
2. *After winning a pinochle tournament, one of the girls went to Wechsler's house for lunch.*
3. *Yvette and Lorge joined the choir after Tom and the rummy player talked them into it.*
4. *Tom shares a desk with the canasta player in math class.*

Clue 1: From these facts we know that Thorndike does not play rummy and that he is likely not Emelia or Yvette. Binet is probably not Emilia or Yvette either.

Clue 2: Thorndike and Binet do not play pinochle. Wechsler does not play pinochle. Therefore, Lorge plays pinochle.

Clue 3: Yvette is not Lorge. Therefore,Yvette is Wechsler and Emelia must be Lorge. Yvette and Lorge do not play rummy. Therefore, Binet plays rummy. Tom must be Thorndike and Antoine is Binet.

Clue 4: Tom does not play canasta. Therefore, he plays solitaire and Yvette plays canasta.

PINOCHLE	RUMMY	CANASTA	SOLITAIRE
(2)	(1)	(4)	•
(2)	•		
•	(3)		
(2)	(3)	•	

Occasionally, a student can use a diagram to help organize and manage the data. In this problem, for example, not only is a chart useful but, from the information, one can produce a diagram which will help in the reasoning/deduction process.

Four old school chums are seated around a fireplace, swapping stories of their childhood days. Their names are Winston, Hrabosky, Jergens, and Scollins, and they make their living as follows: one is a professional assassin; another is a hockey referee; a third is an undercover policeman; and the fourth is a magician.

From the information that follows, determine exactly where each one is sitting and what each does for a living.

1. *Scollins and Jergens have just lit cigars.*
2. *The assassin likes to sit where he can stare directly into the fireplace.*
3. *Hrabosky and Scollins, who is a bachelor, do not have sisters.*
4. *The referee does not smoke.*
5. *Hrabosky is sitting in one of the single chairs with the referee on his left.*
6. *Hrabosky is the policeman's brother-in-law.*
7. *Two of the people are sitting on a sofa which faces the fireplace. There is a single chair to the left of the sofa and one to the right. All the furniture is occupied.*

The activities at the Step Two level in teaching this strategy need not be as difficult as the one above tends to be. Fairly simple ones, such as the following, can also accomplish the objective of teaching students to organize and manage data.

Stella is leaving on the 10:10 bus. Her watch, which is eight minutes fast, says 10:02 when she reaches the terminal. She has:

(a) sixteen minutes to wait;
(b) eight minutes to wait;
(c) missed the bus.

Levin's watch, on the other hand, is nine minutes slow. The 10:10 bus is leaving five minutes late. When Levin reaches the terminal, his watch says 10:09. He has:

(a) missed the bus;
(b) arrived just in time.

Bonita's watch loses three minutes an hour. At 8:10 exactly she sets her watch to the correct time. If the 10:10 bus leaves three minutes late and if Bonita forgets to reset her watch each hour, will she miss the bus or be there for the bus?

Not only do activities like these accustom students to the use of a logical approach and generally make students feel more at ease with moderate to large amounts of information, there is an intangible benefit that develops as well. Because these activities yield to precise solutions, there is a sense of accomplishment, of strong satisfaction, that comes from solving them. While this sense of satisfaction is a common enough occurrence among successful students, it is not among those who need this programme most. Thus, if a sense of accomplishment, a feeling of confidence, can grow along with an ability to organize and manage detail, then this strategy is worth the fairly lengthy time that students and teachers are likely to spend on it.

Divergent Thinking

The chart on p. 109 does not show solid lines inter-connecting this strategy with the others. This is not to imply that divergent thinking is disassociated from the other strategies, or in any way inimical to them, or by any means less important. But, divergent thinking is different. Whereas the other strategies seek to impose sequence and precision and judgement, divergent thinking encourages uninhibited idea production by setting aside judgement and sequence and precision. Whereas the other strategies encourage a logical narrowing of focus until a specific objective is attained, divergent thinking aims at expansion, at a widening of perspective, at impetus toward more and more possibilities rather than fewer and fewer. Data, in the other strategies, are to be controlled. Data, here, are only a springboard.

Yet, the two areas are entirely compatible; in fact, they are essential to each other. Without divergent thinking, there would be few new ideas, very little data to which the other more logical strategies might be applied. Yet, the latter are needed to give functional shape to the ideas produced in the divergent thinking process. Adolescents with learning problems benefit from practice in both areas. The logical strategies help them to organize and manage their thought processes. Divergent thinking makes them capable of producing ideas in quantity. Both are vital to efficient thinking.

The basic purpose of teaching divergent thinking is to develop a flexibility of mind, a capacity for seeing new relationships, generating original ideas, envisioning alternatives, and developing different interpretations. In effect, if the mind were to be seen as a muscle, then the purpose of divergent thinking would be to put it into a healthy condition. This seems to be achieved best by the intellectual calisthenics of *brainstorming*. To brainstorm a problem is to take one like this:

An English city's Underground Commission was losing a fortune through stolen light bulbs. Riders were removing bulbs, often leaving cars in total darkness by the end of a run. Since the commission could not afford more security guards, what do you imagine they did?

and generate a whole series of possible solutions out of which may come at least one that is an ideal solution. Or brainstorming may simply involve a session of idea production for its own sake. A group might take a problem like:

How many ways can you suggest to improve the door to your classroom?

and try to produce the maximum amount of ideas solely for the sake of the exercise.

Teachers are familiar with the concept and basic processes of the brainstorming technique. For purposes of the classroom, however, there are certain features of method which are worth emphasis. Experience underlines the merit of the suggestions that follow:

1. Ideally a brainstorm group numbers six; never less than five nor more than seven.

2. A group *must* function in close physical proximity with every member having a clear sight line to every other member of the group.

3. A group must have a recorder: someone who will jot down the ideas rapidly and in short form.

4. The purpose of a brainstorming session, especially in the initial phases, is to produce a *quantity* of ideas. Quality is not a concern. The group must generate as many ideas as it possibly can.

5. There are no ridiculous ideas; there are only ideas. Usually, this point (with number 4) is the most difficult element to get across to students. The value of the principle is that a ridiculous idea may trigger a useful and reasonable one, as for example, in a brainstorming session on this problem:

   You are about to embark on a six-hour train ride during which you will be in charge of your seven-year-old nephew and your eight-year-old niece. What are some of the things you might do to keep them occupied during the trip?

   One solution offered was to "drag them behind the train," which led quickly to "No! Let them run along beside it!" which, in turn, led to: "Why not let them run around the parking lot at the station stop?" The latter is a reasonable and, certainly, a useful idea (especially true for any adult who has spent six hours on a train with children!).

6. It is essential to *warm up* students first. Give them some mildly challenging "fun" exercises or carry out warm up exercises in the manner of "warm-ups" in dramatic arts classes. Only by warming up will students overcome inhibitions, especially in the early days of Step Two.

   Here are some sample "warm-ups."

   (a) Each student has a blank page and a pencil; the teacher then gives instructions:

   "Everybody draw three squares and then make something out of them. Don't hesitate. Don't think about it. Just *go*!"

   (Repeat immediately with circles, triangles, etc.)

   (b) *Words and Phrases:* Present students with examples of "visualized" words, like these:

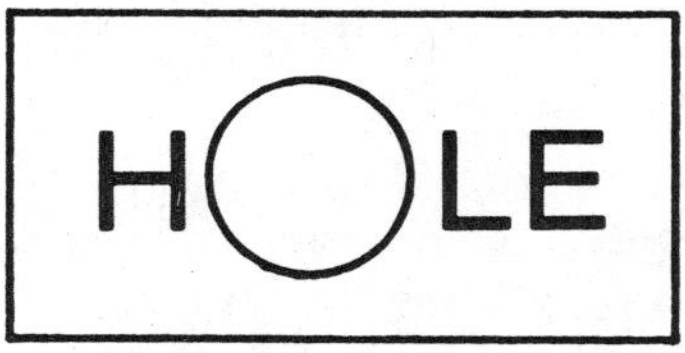

And then invite them to repeat the procedure with words like: bottom, apple, around, few, explosion, rushed, growing, speedy.

(c) A similar process is visualization of phrases. These will likely be familiar to students from puzzle books or similar publications. The idea is to translate the message in each box. e.g.

With a little reflection, students should come up with "pie in the sky," "round of applause," "what goes up must come down." Warm-up activities will involve both interpreting phrases and designing them. (e.g. "man in the moon;" "hold on a second;" "spreading the gospel.")

7. Once students have warmed-up, the first several problems given them should be reasonably easy to "storm;" that is, reasonably in terms of the production of a quantity of ideas. Such problems as the one stated in #5 are fairly easy.

8. At some point, students should become aware of the concept of hitchhiking: how one idea can generate another, as in #5.

9. Also, the idea of elaboration should be emphasized. That is, once a group begins to bog down in the production of ideas, it then takes one of the ideas suggested and builds on it. For example, in #5 one solution invariably suggested is "games." This is an item that can be elaborated on at length.

10. As students become more proficient, the problems should become a little more difficult:

What would be some of the results if our planet were to change so that we had six months of total darkness followed by six months of total light every year?

You have just become a group of writers for a publisher of children's books. Your first task is to produce an auto-alphabet book for children beginning to learn the alphabet. For each letter of the alphabet, invent the name of a car—one not yet in existence. Try to make the names of the cars suggest what the car is like.

11. Some problems should invite research and verification of information. It is easy to see how this one could accomplish that:

    Make a list of twenty-two different things that would result, immediately or eventually, if the prevailing winds in the part of the country where you live suddenly shifted to the opposite direction.

12. At some point, every brainstorming session must have an evaluation. A popular method is to have each group submit its best five answers. These are collated by the teacher and, in a class discussion, the very best few are selected. Often, at this stage, there is a great deal of hitchhiking, elaboration, and even the development of new ideas by the class as a whole.

Brainstorming is useful. It's fun. And it's universally applicable in education. Unfortunately, it's all too frequently ignored. It needn't be.

Given an unlimited budget, unlimited authority, and unlimited technology, what one *improvement would you make to the average school class*room*?*

A Few Final Questions

Just how does one integrate divergent thinking with the other more specifically focussed strategies? Divergent thinking, like identifying starting points and establishing and testing hypotheses is another way *into* a problem. Very often, by brainstorming a range of possibilities prior to actually attempting a solution, students will have a list of hypotheses to test or a series of options to explore systematically. In the activities following, for example, there are several approaches one might take in each one. By first producing a list of possibilities through brainstorming, one, then, has a number of options to pursue systematically and logically.

Which is the odd one out?

BEAR
FEAR
HEAR
TEAR
WEAR

Which word in the bottom column comes next in this series?

FIX LIE TAN TEA WET

NEW
LET
TIE
WAY
EVE
SHY

What word completes the fourth column?

183	*153*	*167*	*193*
122	*233*	*176*	*172*
DIE	*CAD*	*BEG*	

Is there a special sequence with which one should approach the strategies in this programme? A particular sequence is preferable simply because it allows a teacher to introduce each strategy in a way that students will find manageable. If all strategies were to be presented simultaneously, students would likely turn to those avoidance behaviours which the programme is designed to help circumvent. But the determination of what sequence to follow is at the discretion of individual teachers. One point worth noting is that, whereas each of the more logical strategies will receive a very specific emphasis in turn, divergent thinking seems to have more effect, if it is continued on a regular basis over an entire school year.

How much time does it take to cover the whole programme? There is no absolute figure here. Strategies should be presented at a rate which classroom teachers see to be ideal for their students. The objective is that the students learn the processes, however long that takes.

Any pitfalls to avoid? Only the danger of allowing the programme to become taskbound. Students enjoy the activities at Step Two, especially, and it is tempting to let the programme settle there. The activities are only means of teaching a thinking process, an effective strategy, and that should be their sole purpose. It is even advisable most of the time to depreciate the importance of the answer.

Is there any more research to substantiate the programme? Several pieces of research have been mentioned in this book and, at this writing, two long-term projects are under way. Nevertheless, it is almost impossible to measure this type of cognitive training in terms that completely satisfy the demands of research. Numbers alone cannot reflect the impact of awakening the cognitive potential in adolescents with learning problems. Once they think more efficiently, the results show, not just in academic terms, but in behavioural and social-life terms as well. Teaching efficient thinking establishes momentum, and once momentum is established, these students will begin to teach themselves.

Where do I find more activities for practice at Step Two? Many teachers write their own, using samples, such as those in this Chapter, as models. Students are often very effective writers of activities. In fact, designing material is very often an ideal activity in itself. However, there does come a point when energy and time run out, and it is necessary to turn to an outside source. The most useful sources known to this writer are *Thinklab* and *Thinklab 2,* © 1974 and 1976, Science Research Associates, Toronto, and *Insight 1* and *Insight 2* © 1980, Methuen Publications. All the examples used in this book are taken from these publications.

Can adolescents with learning problems really do the activities in Step Two that are presented in this chapter? Every activity in this chapter has been class-tested and successfully completed by most of the students whose work has been reprinted in earlier chapters—students such as Sergio, Stuart, and Stanford. Students can indeed do these activities, but as always, they need their teachers.

They need their teachers to structure a time frame for them, a time frame that does not impose a limit; they need to have the activities structured in a sequence of increasing difficulty, with—obviously—the easier examples first; they need to work *with* their teachers so that undeveloped reading skills do not impose a barrier. A teacher should feel free to begin an activity by doing several readings of it with his students, if there is any anxiety about their comprehending it. Above all, teachers are needed for encouragement, for help, for resource, for guidance. If students are simply left on their own with the activities in Step Two, they *will* flounder. Worse, such an approach will only make the process task-bound. These are activities that are designed to involve both teachers and students in a strategic, cognitive process—a process that, again with the help of the teacher, will have ever-widening applications.

Bibliography

Feuerstein, R., *The Dynamic Assessment of Retarded Performers,* Baltimore: Univ. Park Press, 1979.

Feuerstein, R., *Instrumental Enrichment,* Baltimore: Univ. Park Press, 1980.

Hallahan, D.P. *et al.*, "Selective attention and cognitive tempo of low achieving and high achieving sixth grade males," *Perceptual Motor Skills,* 1973, 36, 579-583.

Havertape, J.F., "The communication function in learning disabled adolescents: A study of verbalized self-instructions." Unpublished doctoral dissertation, Univ. of Arizona, 1976.

Keogh, B., "Hyperactivity and learning disorders: Review and Speculation," *Exceptional Children,* 1971, 38, 101-110.

Messer, S., "The effect of anxiety over intellectual performance on reflection-impulsivity in children, *Child Development,* 1970, 31, 723-735.

Wilcox, E., "Identifying characteristics of the NH adolescent," in Anderson, L.E. (Ed.), *Helping the Adolescent With the Hidden Handicap.* Belmont, Calif.: Fearon, 1970.

CHAPTER 9

ESTABLISHING EFFECTIVE AND REASONABLE CLASS-ROOM MANAGEMENT

Memorandum to all teachers of G9K
From: ABP
12 June:
Re: Planning for fall semester

As you are aware, G9K was placed in our school on an experimental basis this year. This was our first experience with students like this, and you are no doubt aware that our collective success has been somewhat dubious. Therefore, pursuant to our meeting on this matter and in order to plan for next year, I am asking each teacher of G9K to prepare a brief report, unstructured and anecdotal where necessary, to help next year's teachers of this class plan the appropriate style of management for these students.

ABP

THIS MEMO came from the desk of a secondary school principal widely recognized for his ability to combine authority and efficiency with reason and sympathy. By his own admission, however, he was baffled by the students about whom he was writing. No less so than his teachers. Until the arrival of G9K, both he and his staff had been comfortably rooted in that tradition which holds secondary school to be a subject-specialized preparatory level for university. They had had little or no experience with students for whom this tradition has neither meaning nor value.

Not that they were without the experience to deal with disciplinary situations when necessary. Every teacher confronts these problems no matter what kind of students he teaches. What bewildered this staff was the *nature* of the behaviour problems in G9K: the frequency, the intensity, and, most of all, the ineffectiveness of traditional measures in responding to them. These students did not seem to care a whit about threatened withdrawal of privileges, for they rarely took advantage of them anyway; they were inured to punishment and oblivious to authoritative anger. Even the inevitable result of too much misbehaviour, namely *failure*, seemed of no concern to them. After a year with G9K, it was apparent to their teachers that very little was available in the traditional canon for managing their behaviour.

The principal's memo, probably because it was so unspecific, elicited a kaleidoscope of reaction. Interestingly, the responses reveal as much about the teachers as they do about G9K. This is a significant issue in classroom management of most adolescents with learning difficulties, for the attitude of the teacher is easily as important as the attitude of the students.

Some responses demonstrated the inevitable truth that there are often one or two teachers in any school who probably should not become responsible for a class like G9K.

> *Thank you for this opportunity to say that, for next year, count me out. My contract requires me to teach geography, not to play warden, custodian, babysitter, mollycoddler, social worker, arbitrator, referee, and all-round inquisitor-cum-entertainment director for a bunch of undeserving types who ignore all our efforts, defy all our rules, and reject all our values. Why do we waste our time with people who don't even want to be here?*

In slightly more florid prose, another staff member revealed equally strong feelings.

> *Given the intensity and the extent of our negative experiences with this group, and in due recognition of the values to which this institution subscribes, I would deem it advisable, indeed urgently necessary, that before the little bastards breed and reproduce their like, they be exterminated as hastily and humanely as possible.*

Both of the above teachers were experienced practitioners of the art and both had long-standing reputations for excellence. Until G9K, they had regarded their role exclusively as effective teachers of their *subjects*. Their articulate cynicism shows the extent of their frustration with students who do not respond to this approach.

Yet another response was bewilderment. The experience of teaching a class like G9K can leave some professionals still searching for an appropriate method of management even after a whole year.

> *I am at a total loss to advise anyone. These students hated history and, as a consequence, me. I got nowhere with them. There was no trust, no dialogue, no discipline, no respect, no learning. After twelve years as a teacher, they make me wonder if I belong here.*

Yelling and screaming are counterproductive. Throughout the first term I found myself reacting to their noise with yet more noise. My response only set up a chain-reaction: the louder I got, the louder they became. But then quietness doesn't work either. There must be some means of capturing and maintaining their attention without using extreme measures. When you find out what it is, tell me.

Still others showed that they had become caught up in dealing with the specific personalities in G9K. This is a frequent outcome but usually a counter-productive one, for it obscures the teacher's view. Reaction to one or two individuals can prejudice the teacher's attitude to the whole group.

The essence of control is in dealing with G9K's personality dynamics. Ferguson T. and Rodney B. hate each other; they must be seated well apart. Luigi S. is in constant motion. He must be seated in the rear where he'll not disturb anyone. And whatever the affliction is that controls Luigi's limbs also has possession of Fergie's mouth. Even when he is not dominating a class discussion (rare occurrence, the latter) he is talking to himself. Seat him between Ruthie and Reenie McB. They seem to be oblivious to absolutely everything anyway.

Ferguson T. cannot remember to bring both his books and a pen. Irene G. cannot distinguish English literature class from English composition class. Basil G. and Ruthie McB. lost every single book on the course at one time or another. So did Ray P. who also lost my books! Griffith H. has showed up for English when he should be in math class on an average of at least once weekly. Somehow, we have to get a system which makes automatic routine easier to follow.

Certainly, it is essential to be aware of the individual personality quirks in a group like G9K, but to concentrate on them reduces the long-term potential for establishing effective group management. To react in a very specific way to certain students whose behaviour draws attention usually serves only to reinforce that behaviour. Worse still, the teacher who is caught up in personalities is prone to responding inconsistently to the same behaviours from different students: a potentially disastrous pattern.

Finally, there were the inevitable attempts to attach the behaviour of G9K to causes outside the school environment.

I am aware that these students do not get enough sleep. I'm certain some of them don't have enough to eat—or, at least, they don't eat properly. Physically, they don't have the energy to learn. Another thing I've noticed is that they are never home. Since I live in the neighbourhood and see them in the streets all night long, I know they can't be studying or doing homework.

Ferguson T's common-law stepfather (Is that the proper term?) told me in one of our many consultations that my (our) job is to teach, and if he (Ferguson) "ain't learnin'," it's my (our) fault. I was also told that Ferguson's behaviour "ain't no different here than 'tis to home," so why am I upset? If there is no support for decent behaviour in the home situation, how can we be expected to enforce it here at school?

And thus the responses ran. When a group of intelligent and articulate professionals, committed to an idea about education, are thrown into a situation which seemingly contradicts that idea, they can be expected to respond with intense feeling. In their reports, these teachers were being what teachers are first: human beings. They were using the opportunity to vent their spleens through anger, humour, cynicism, and even confessions of guilt and resignation. Only non-teachers or, more precisely, only those who have never experienced a G9K would presume to criticize this very human and very natural response. The principal later confided that he had expected such reactions and, indeed, had set out to provoke them in order to release the collective tension he had perceived.

A Co-ordinated Policy of Behaviour Management

Premise One

The principal also expected some worthwhile commentary once the air was clear. He knew that his staff members were professionals and he knew that teachers will keep searching for solutions in the face of even the most overwhelming and depressing odds. He knew that, from his staff, he could eventually draw the philosophical and practical basis of a behaviour management policy for G9K. Interestingly, the very first premise in what became the behaviour management philosophy for G9K came from the same person whose feelings toward G9K seemed most virulent. After the luxury of purging himself, he proceeded, in his invariably cynical fashion, to make a crucial point.

Be that as it may, G9K is here. (Given their achievement they are probably here to stay, God forbid!) And that makes them our responsibility. If all their learning and behaviour problems were environmental and familial we could fill the place with social workers; if their problems were all emotional, we could fill up with psychiatrists; if it's diet, then nutritionists could

> *solve the problem. But helpful as these people might be, the learning and behaviour problems of G9K are our business. No airlift of outside expertise will solve them. We must do it.*

There is a normal temptation in education to shuffle off the responsibility for solving problems to the nearest available agent of supposed expertise. Almost invariably, solutions to generalized problems, such as those caused by G9K, involve recommendations to solicit outside help. Once the help arrives, a common reaction is to leave the solution entirely to the new aid and turn to other things. Very few people welcome the responsibility of a G9K, but it is a responsibility that, once given, must be accepted. Otherwise, all the teacher's actions, reactions, relationships, plans, and policies with that class are coloured by the attitude that the situation is temporary. If there is to be any progress toward effective management of a class like G9K, there must first be commitment from all the teachers.

Premise Two

From the teacher who questioned her own worth and ability in the initial paragraphs of her report came a second philosophical premise on which sound teaching and management practices must be based.

> *Still, when I think about it, why should G9K behave? What's in it for them? Here they are in a school, indeed in a world, of successful people and the only thing they have in common is their lack of success. They are the "out-group." What's the point of obeying the rules of a system that does them no good—in their eyes, anyway? They're almost compelled to misbehave. The only way we're going to get anywhere with them will be if they see some purpose to the whole exercise. For them, there has to be some reason for being here. We've got to make them participants in their own education. Somehow, we've got to show them that there's joy in the morrow.*

Adolescents, particularly the G9K variety, have long passed the stage where they will accept the value and purpose of education as a matter of faith. It is inevitable that these students will doubt and then resent the system that seems to offer success to everyone but themselves. Add an environment in which those comparisons are obvious, include the collective psyche of adolescence wherein peer pressure is irresistible, and problems become almost unavoidable.

In this matter, the administrative placement design for adolescents with learning and behaviour problems seems to make little difference. Very often, if the members of a G9K are scattered across several successful classes, the behaviour management problems seem to be less urgent, simply because whatever difficulties they generate are diffused across a wider area. But, if their learning problems are genuine, the likelihood of these being remediated in this arrangement is probably reduced, so that, in effect, their real needs (i.e. learning needs) are being sacrificed to a surface expediency (i.e. behaviour control). Even so, there is still a significant percentage of these adolescents who will continue their behaviour patterns unabated. Some, especially those whose personalities are strong, can effectively alter the character of a hitherto successful group. Then there are those who, because the contrast of their own situation is made so sharp by the success of their classmates, simply drop out.

On the other hand, collecting all the G9K type of student into one class can often mean that a situation is created in which there is mutual support for expression of resentment and for inappropriate behaviour. To a certain extent, behaviour problems in the context of a G9K seem less serious, partly because there is often so much of it and partly because it is expected. Indeed, if a school administration makes the dubious decision to designate a G9K class as "behavioural," there is a great temptation among the students to rise to the label they have been given.

The point is that such students will never become participants in their education unless they see some purpose in it. Years of defeat have created a sense of learned resistance and learned helplessness that can only be interrupted by success. A sense of momentum must be generated and maintained.

Premise Three

From the first two premises, namely the necessity of professional commitment, not mere acceptance, and the necessity of building momentum through "joy in the morrow," came the philosophical basis of a management philosophy for G9K. What was still needed, however, was an element that was somehow as functional as it was philosophic, something that could tie the teachers of G9K together and create for them, too, a sense of momentum. Such an element grew from this contribution.

> *One thing I observed about G9K merits our very serious consideration. In first term, they came to my class daily at 2:45 p.m. and I dreaded their coming. Some of them were uncontrollable, some were asleep. Some came with books, some without. Some were able to work, others had simply tuned out. And everyone, without exception, wanted to go to the washroom. In second term, I had them at 9:00 a.m., and, frankly, it was almost pleasant. No intellectual excitement mind you, but their behaviour was—well, manageable. My classroom rules are few, reasonable, and simple (at least I think so!) and it was no effort to enforce them. In fact, after a few weeks, the whole thing was automatic. They would enter, select a pen from my "special jar," sit down, place unneeded books under their*

> *desks, and begin to work on the practice drill I use to begin every lesson.*
>
> *And everything else flowed from there. My lesson was always short; they always participated. I discourage blurting out; that was no problem. I encourage taking of notes from the chalkboard; they all did so. It was almost—well, pleasant!*
>
> *Now here's the crunch. I don't change my style between 9:00 a.m. and 2:45 p.m. Then why did it work so well in the morning and not at all in the afternoon? (Nothing worked in the afternoon.) I refuse to believe that G9K changes that much on its own, over six hours. Somehow we must be the ones who change them. Can we examine this possibility?*

To a significant degree, the counter-productive behaviour of many adolescents with learning problems is a result of the very way in which most secondary schools function. The rotating timetable system, ideal for moving groups of students from subject expert to subject expert over the course of a day, has an undesirable set of effects on these students. As they shift from classroom to classroom, there develops an accelerating sense of dislocation and displacement, particularly if the time spent in each area is short. Students must shift gears intellectually and emotionally, as well as physically, in a rotating timetable, and adolescents with learning problems find this very hard to do. It takes a long time for them to adjust to each new environment, each new set of expectations, each new mind-set—a longer time than is usually available. As any successful student is quick to acknowledge, winning in the game of "school" is, at least partly, a consequence of knowing how to respond to the changing rules as one rotates from class to class. Students with learning and behaviour problems cannot—or will not—play this way. A G9K does not seem to be able to accommodate the variation in teachers' management demands, work expectations, and teaching styles. The result is an honest confusion on their part to which they respond by increasingly intense acting out as the day—indeed the term—progresses. If, for example, their first and second teachers have very specific demands for classroom-entering behaviour and the third has none at all, the *fourth* teacher they meet, no matter what his "rules," will face their confusion. If some teachers give homework and some do not, then incomplete assignments are a certainty. Certain teachers insist on note-taking; others do not. The result: confusion and resentment. When there is no general policy for attending with books, for being excused from class, for classroom-entering processes, for dealing with homework, for all those necessary bits and pieces that are essential for the practical function of a classroom, the result is, inevitably, a *school-generated* creeping chaos. The teacher who has no policies at all will have chaos because it is—to the students—permitted, indeed invited. The teacher who has policies will have chaos because it is impossible to implement them in isolation. And, as all teachers recognize, once general disruption is established in a G9K, it only gets worse.

A popular administrative response to this phenomenon has been to create segregated class units, usually labelled with a euphemism like "modified" class, or "adjusted," or "resource," or "approved." The idea is that behaviour-problem students will spend all or part of their day with a single teacher. The process can be successful, if that single teacher is effective in this design. The disadvantages, however, are that such segregation increases these students' sense of isolation from the mainstream and frequently denies them the breadth of academic experience a school can offer. Such a special unit, moreover, is all too susceptible to becoming a discard pile for all those discomforting problems that no one wants to handle. The segregated unit class should be strictly a placement of last resort. For the majority of adolescents with learning and behaviour problems, it is possible to organize a much more effective system of classroom management. What it requires is the co-operation of the administration and *all* teachers involved.

Since these adolescents respond favourably to a clear, consistent, school-wide policy, one that is reasonable but effectively and universally implemented,[1] it seems eminently sensible to organize and put in place such a system wherever G9K classes attend. The idea is, simply, that, with the active leadership and support of the administration, all teachers invoke a common policy for each of those classroom functions which can either smooth the path or make it impossible. If all teachers follow a similar policy for classroom-entering behaviour (e.g. students in every class enter, open notebooks directly, and begin a short piece of work written on the chalkboard), then classroom-entering, that crucial first step which usually establishes the tone for the remainder of the lesson, will gradually diminish as a problem. A class like G9K will become accustomed to the idea that there is a specific pattern in every class, and they will follow it. The same can be established for a homework policy, a "bringing-books" policy, an "excuse from the classroom" policy—in fact, just about every aspect of classroom management a school may deem important.

Granted, the system does smack of "rules," of a pattern that marked the discipline procedures of an earlier part of this century, a pattern that most present-day teachers would prefer to avoid. But careful examination of the idea shows that this is not a case of making lists of rules for their own sake. Rather, it is a structure that frees the teachers and their students from the constant struggle of wills, the constant confusion, and the constant comparisons that inevitably cast someone into an unfavourable light. What such a set of common policies does is to establish

[1]Readers are again urged to refer to the research by Rutter et al. on this subject. See p. 46.

momentum—behavioural momentum—a pervading ethos that gives both students and teachers a sense of unity and common purpose. Empirical evidence, common sense, and now research validate the strength of the approach. All it requires is that every teacher and the school administration participate.

For G9K and their teachers, the decision to establish this co-ordinated approach as the baseline feature of a policy of classroom management worked wonders in the next term. For the teachers, it gave initial direction to the sense of commitment they knew was necessary. Further, it made "joy in the morrow" a reality much easier to bring about, for the momentum created by the teamwork stimulated better work from the students. Communication among staff improved. For example, teachers found homework easier to administer by agreeing that certain subjects held precedence on Mondays and Wednesdays, the remainder on Tuesdays and Thursdays, with Fridays and the weekend being "free." The previously high profile of serious problem students diminished because the response by teachers to their inappropriate behaviour was consistent across the team. (The latter feature was of great help to a few of the teachers for whom classroom control was not a strong point and who had found that their disciplinary measures, even though identical to those used by another teacher, often produced less effective results.) The truancy rate decreased dramatically, probably because the students gradually began to believe that school existed for them too. Above all, the general attitude of the students, their demeanour, their response to the daily teaching-learning exchange, even their appearance improved significantly. Although not one teacher could describe it precisely, everyone seemed to respond to a prevailing ethos of order, reason, and common purpose.

In short, the system was beneficial to everyone. Behaviour had become less and less of an issue, so that education could take over. Not that the road was without bumps. As with anything new for adolescents with learning and behaviour difficulties, the very first stages were depressingly unsuccessful. There was, typically, a barrier of "We done this awready!" in the students and "It'll never work!" in several teachers. Some staff members misinterpreted the concept of teaming and tried to operate as though each was a clone-like cutout of the other. It took time for them to realize that individual teaching styles need not be affected. The administration found it had to alter the timetable to build in opportunity for regular meetings of the team, gatherings which soon proved to be vital to the whole process. Ultimately, however, the teachers of G9K (by this time the class had become G10K) found their policy an unqualified success. It gave them what all teachers look for: reasonable peace and the opportunity to teach.

Students Have More Need of Models Than Critics

It would be wrong to leave the impression that G9K, their colleagues, their teachers, and the principal had discovered some sort of utopia. No one challenged the truth that things were immeasurably improved, but life, students, teachers, and schools being what they are, there were problems from time to time. There are always students who begin the day in a foul temper; the same is true for teachers. (Would that they could avoid being in this state on the same day!) Then there are the misunderstandings, the mistakes, the misinterpretations that are inescapable when teachers and adolescents come together on an intense, daily basis. Recognizing, nevertheless, that the vast majority of so-called discipline problems are entirely preventable, the same principal who had invited opinions from the teachers of G9K also turned to the students for their point of view. His hope was to elicit some practical commentary that would support his intent to develop more effective *individual* teacher behaviour. It took two weeks of regular visits before G9K accepted the sincerity of his purpose, but the results were well worth his efforts. Here, unaltered to preserve the flavour—and the wisdom— is their advice.[1]

Ironically, several students first chose the opportunity to do exactly what their teachers had done: let off some steam.

> *If I was our teacher, I'd quit. You guys got to be nuts to stick this out. There's no way I'd put up with the stuff in here.*

> *The first thing I wood do is dig a hole in the socer field. And then I wood burry Fergisen T. up to his nek then I wood march the hole school singl file over his g.d.tung you shood have to sit in front of that meatball for a hole year!*

> *I'd buy ear plugs for all my students so they wouldn't have ear damage when I yell. That's what teacher's do isn't it: yell? Even though it just makes their students worse.*

> *To begin with I would try to hide my prejidice at classes like us because kids can tell when teachers dont like them Just because we dont suck up like the other kids in this school it doesn't mean we're less than they are. If I was a teacher I'd give my students fair deal no matter who they are.*

There is some bitterness in these comments and, although the

[1]The specific request was that they advise what they would do, if they were teachers of G9K. Some responses were written, others were recorded; hence the variations in spelling accuracy.

students are less articulate than their teachers were, the feelings expressed are no less intense. If one looks back to the initial positions of the teachers and compares them with those above, it is obvious that the potential for an adversarial situation is very strong: another reason for establishing some kind of co-ordinated management policy, the momentum of which will carry both teachers and students beyond this trap.

It is quite possible for both teachers and students to move past these first dangerous stages of distrust. The teachers showed it in their subsequent reflections on what is needed for a G9K. The students did the same in theirs. The comments of both groups make it quite apparent that teachers and students realize, ultimately, that so much of the confrontation, the difficulty, the perceived injustice, the presumed mistreatment, and the supposed lack of attention and concern is simply unnecessary. It can be avoided most of the time by reason and common sense. In support of this view, no statement was more profound than the laboriously written one that follows. It came from Danny, a quiet and very slow-moving boy whose impenetrable calm and infinite patience was often mistaken for dullness.

> *A teacher cant be a teacher unless he got a sens of humer. Teachers are alway too awfull serius. Everthing they do they always take themself so terribl serius we like teachers that laugh not outloud all the time but insid themself and we dont like the ones who ack like God made them and their subjek before He mad anything els. Like Fergie he says he bets Mr.________('s) wife and kids got to follouw him aroun and clap and bow and cheere and even stan at atthenshin when he gos to the bathrom cause hes so dam important Thats no way to be a teacher. If all the facs in one subjek are so important howcom one teacher dont know anything about another subjeck? Like our science teacher she dont know nothig about history and vissa verssa but we are spozed to know both so if we do does that make us mor edducated than them? If I was a teacher Id set down ever day and tell mysef two things one that im not more important than anybody els and two hows my subjek going to help the studens for ten years from now. If I did this then I wont go waco over little things.*

Although Danny's syntax and spelling may be suspect, his perception should be applauded. There is no more common pitfall nor one more deadly for a teacher than taking one's self and, by natural consequence, the content of one's subject, too seriously. There is no outcome more destructive than when teachers lose sight of *why* they do what they do. There is nothing more depressing than a classroom in which a teacher has no "joy in the morrow." Not that the whole process should be dismissed as a lark. Rather, it is a case of simply accepting that things do go wrong, that the world is not perfect—especially in a classroom. It is a case of recognizing that people do live a full life without knowing the atomic weight of mercury, the date of the Treaty of Ghent, the niceties of prime numbers, or even scoring 8.2 on a reading test! Granted the day-to-day demands of teaching adolescents with learning problems can cloud one's perspective. When this factor is compounded by the sheer volume of work most teachers put into a class of problem students, it is no surprise that the sense of humour may diminish. But, if there is ever to be a positive atmosphere in a classroom, it is essential to acknowledge Danny's advice. It is what a student does, long after he has forgotten the details of a subject, that determines how well he was taught. And how well he was taught will as likely as not depend on whether there was "joy in the morrow" for his teachers as well as himself.

Danny's classmates matched his philosophical offering with comments that were more practical in their content but certainly just as illuminating for teachers interested in effective classroom control.

> *First off, if I'm the teacher, my students are gonna know what's what right up front. None of this making up rules as I go along and having some rules for some of them and some for others.*
>
> *Second, I'm not gonna make my students do stuff unless I'm geared up for it. Like for example if I make them bring books every day then we're gonna use the books. Otherwise why the—why should they bring them.*
>
> *Third I'm not gonna come apart if somebody goofs off once or twice. I mean everybody should get a second chance. After that I stomp on their heads. Even Fergie would go along with that.*
>
> *Fourth I'm gonna make it my business to say something good about my students instead of always crapping on them. I mean you can catch more flies with honey than vinegar.*
>
> *P.S. Sir, are you gonna let Mrs.__________ read this? We gotta get together and do something about her before it's too late.*

The preceding is from Sal, an outspoken, bumptious fifteen year old whose utter lack of concern for his appearance had earned him the nickname of "Swamp." His was always the loudest voice of protest in G9K and the first to be heard in the face of perceived injustice. What Sal lacked in tact, however, he made up in perception—at least this time. Students who find it difficult to manage themselves want clear, consistent structures. They want a system that is not only just but one that they perceive as just. And, above all, they want reward and praise for work well done. These are not excessive demands; they are no more than the teachers would ask, were the position reversed.

A further tribute to reason—and a stinging refutation of the belief that the G9K type of student cares nothing for his education—was delivered by none other than Fergie himself.

> *Kids know when their teachers are goofing off. I mean—like—some teachers never prepare, right? And they think we don't notice, 'cause we don't care, right? But we know. We know when they're just fillin' in time, Like—I mean—like how many crossword puzzles do you have to do before you figure it out. Maybe they don't know what to do with us but—I mean—like—we're in school so why not give us school work? You want to know why we screw around? Cause we got nothin' to do, that's why!*
>
> *Hey, but—like—that's not everybody. I mean, take Ms ______. Like—in her class do we ever put out! I mean she's got work and everything, every day! Like there's always stuff on the board, and then we get a lesson-thing, and then more work. And we got this ton of notes.*
>
> *Nobody messes around in Ms ______'s class. And—like—it's not just that she's OK and all that. I mean—Jeez—she teaches math! Who wants to do math? But I mean—like—you're doin' somethin' in that class, man. Like—it's like you're learning something!*

Need any more be said?

Finally, from the student who inveighed against the "prejidice" she saw as a problem for herself and her classmates came a statement that neatly counter-balanced her initial criticism.

> *One thing I'd do is be around to talk to us kids. Most of us we get a hassle from our parents cause they never understand what we want, but teachers they can talk to you in a kind of way your parents can't. Like teachers don't have to care if you made your bed or if you smoke up, or who you date and all that so they can talk to you straighter. Like it's not so personal (Is this clear?) I don't mean buddy-buddy stuff. We jump all over teachers who do that and they get laughed at too. I mean straight talk after school and times like that. That's when I like teachers best.*

In this brief treatise from Lindy, there are at least a dozen seminar topics for teachers. Her basic premise, that teachers should be available, is one that most of the profession embraces fully. Teachers enjoy outside-class informal interchange as much as their students. It solves problems, breaks down barriers, and establishes rapport. It allows for an intimacy of contact that the implicit stresses of more formal situations prohibit.

It is a time when teachers can accomplish their most effective classroom management too. Rather than deal fully with a high-profile, high-intensity behaviour situation at the moment of its occurrence, teachers often find it more productive to control it temporarily and then effect an ultimate resolution when the tension has dissipated—and when the likelihood of reasonable discussion is increased. If punishment is necessary, if counselling is advisable, if a misunderstanding must be settled, it is far more effective to attempt it at a time when peer pressure is less likely to stimulate defiance and when the teacher is less likely to be in a state of high dudgeon.

The fact that Lindy warns off teachers from becoming too "buddy-buddy" is also advice worth heeding. Individual classroom management can never be achieved by attempts to befriend the class. Genuine and lasting relationships between teachers and certain of their students do indeed occur. But to force the intimacy and affection that characterizes true friendship causes more difficulties for a teacher of problem students than there are benefits. True friendship cannot be manufactured. These students tend to be very uncomfortable and to lose respect when an authority figure, usually somewhat older, makes overtures that are inconsistent with what they perceive as a teacher's real role. They already have friends from their own milieu. What they expect from their teachers is reason, compassion, encouragement, understanding, and a sense of direction. They do not expect perfection but they expect a best effort and, if this is what they perceive, then effective and reasonable classroom management will follow.

And for Further Consideration

Use organized seating arrangements

The majority of management problems that develop in an individual classroom are ones that can be prevented by careful organization and long-range planning on the part of the teacher. The use of a specific assigned seating arrangement, for example, can be very helpful. It is useful in preventing much of the disorder that can develop at classroom-entering times and which often sets the tone for the remainder of the class. A seating plan can be used to keep apart those inevitable personality combinations whose mere proximity can generate disruption in ever-widening circles. Class "performers," when deliberately seated on the periphery, are often inhibited by the lack of an easily accessible audience. It is simpler to channel the irrepressive, hyperactive student into productive activity if the teacher can be close to him. And, most important of all, a seating plan can be instrumental in contributing to momentum. Very often, classes like G9K are smaller than the norm and do not fill a classroom. If the students spread randomly throughout the room, the resulting clumps of empty desks effectively shut down any potential for that sense of cohesiveness and belonging which carries a group beyond the problems of management. Students need to be seated so that they can become a *class*. Once a group feels itself to be a unit and feels that it is accomplishing something, it tends through its own momentum to control some of the counter-productive behaviour caused by peer pressure.

Design a positive environment

Very few teachers of adolescents with learning problems would dispute the statement that these students are exceptionally responsive to their immediate environment. Since this factor can have either positive or negative implications, it is unfortunate that so many teachers of adolescents, particularly those in secondary school, dismiss the crucial factor of environment as the province of elementary schools. As a consequence, most secondary classrooms are as sterile as storage rooms and just about as interesting. Bulletin board displays, if used at all, are often hoary with dust and hang in tattered tribute to a burst of energy never repeated. Huge spaces of wall stare blankly at students. Even chalkboards over time become forbidding. On the other hand, in those classrooms where effort and creativity have made the place attractive, students not only recognize—albeit silently—that the teacher has made the effort on their behalf, but they also feel that they *belong*. This is not fanciful speculation. Adolescents with learning and behaviour problems are responsive to a momentum-generating environment. They need it for that impetus toward the development of a group sense.

Organize group projects

A teacher can do a great deal to promote the sense of belonging. Any class project, for example, to which every student contributes and which has a specific concrete outcome that the students themselves can point to, will do much to bring them together. Any school activity, campaign, or undertaking which these students join will be instrumental. However, it is the teacher who must encourage, coax, cajole, and, indeed, structure events, so that these students will participate. They have perceived themselves as the "out-group" for so long that an extra push is needed. This must come from their teachers.

> *One of the popular books in Canada for adolescents who are deemed to have "reading problems" has long been a quasi-fictional rendering of a bit of Canadian history. The story of the Donnellys, an Irish immigrant family killed by vigilantes in the late 1800's, has been documented in scholarly fashion by a number of writers. The version that appeals to students is by T.P. Kelley,[1] an account of questionable veracity, gratuitously violent, entirely controversial, and almost impossible to put down, even by the most reluctant reader.*

---

[1]Kelley, T.P. *The Black Donnellys*, Modern Canadian Library, 1974.

Like most teachers of special classes, I was desperate for anything that would encourage my students to read, but I was equally concerned about the quality of "The Black Donnellys." *G9K and I compromised—at my insistence—on a study of this documentary-novel in which each student contributed to a "special-edition" magazine, that might have been published in 1880, to explain to the world what really happened to the Donnellys.*

Each student was assigned a topic. The litany of protest was overcome by writing during class time, so that I could be monitor, editor, chief encourager, and, in some cases, writer of the opening sentence to get things started. The final product was typed, duplicated, collated, and bound in cheap plastic folders, complete with a cover.

To G9K, the sight of over 100 copies of their magazine, only a week later (important point, the latter), was electrifying. It was their *work in print. Something* they *had done. The principal was summoned and presented with a copy. Every one of their teachers received one. So did every one perceived to be a dignitary. The remainder were presented to parents on parents' night (except for twelve copies which Fergie sold to a local bookstore!).*

It was not a literary achievement, but it had a profound effect in bringing G9K together as a unit. Of course, there were a few minor problems. For a week after, G9K refused to do anything but congratulate themselves, not just in my class but in everyone else's. And the one boy who had adamantly refused to participate was driven even further away. For everyone else, it was a project that had brought them together. More important for my management and teaching concerns, it had brought them together with me. *Not that life with G9K was perfect ever after; but it certainly was more pleasant. By sharing, we had crossed a barrier.*

Avoid the counter-productive

Earlier in this chapter, G9K indicated quite clearly that their respect diminishes for any teacher who uses the "yell" mode to establish order. And how correct they are. Yelling, screaming, or nagging—they are all relatives on a scale—merely degrades a teacher's position and serves only to reduce his authority rather than establish it. Certainly, a teacher will raise his voice from time to time, will lose his temper, will explode in loud anger. These are human responses to difficult and stressful situations, and students understand and respect humanity in their teachers. What they do not accept—and with reason—is the high pitch, high intensity mode on a constant daily basis. Authority is relative to quality of function, not to volume. Nor does authority come about through measures that students perceive as unjust or needlessly punitive. Niggling measures, such as the time-honoured practice of making students write out lines, work against the teacher, for they only breed resentment in the students pliant enough to obey and dangerous defiance in those with the determination to dig in their heels. Even more foolish is the practice of arbitrarily punishing an entire class simultaneously for, inevitably, the innocent are swept in with the guilty and are invited, therefore, to join with them for future endeavours.

Not that punishment should be avoided if and when it is appropriate. If students know the rules and are aware of the boundaries, then they also know when these have been transgressed. If transgressions are not dealt with, then it is better to have no rules at all. Students—those with learning problems and those without—expect rules to be enforced. What they also expect in the process is reason and appropriate response. A teacher who sets reasonable—and few—rules and reacts to transgressions of them in what is perceived to be a consistent and fair manner, a teacher who disciplines himself against immediate and explosive reaction to isolated incidents of bad behaviour, a teacher who acknowledges his own humanity and that of his students is a teacher for whom classroom management is less crucial than learning. In the last analysis, the behavioural tone that develops in an individual classroom is the product of the teacher's own behaviour attitude: his response to the question, "Why am I here?"

A matter of attitude

The teacher who conducts himself in a manner that shows he is prepared for confrontation with a G9K will always be thoroughly tested. So will the teacher who pretends there are no problems, who ignores unacceptable behaviour and justifies it as self-expression. Disappointment will weigh on the teacher who conceives his role primarily as teacher of English, or science, or mathematics, or history, instead of as teacher of *students* who happen to be studying English, or science, or mathematics, or history. Most students will distrust the teacher with a Messiah complex or, even worse, take advantage of him. As Fergie once put it, to justify a particularly aberrative piece of behaviour after several weeks of exemplary—for him—conduct: "You can't be perfect *all* the time! Jeez—like, I mean, even Jesus only got eleven out of twelve!" Adolescents with learning and behaviour problems will respond to the reasonable demands of teachers with common sense, firmness, and compassion. These students know in their hearts—and in their heads—that, for them, their teachers are the key. What they want, most of all, is for the teachers to realize it too.

ANSWER KEY

The following are the solutions to the activities given as examples in Chapters 7 and 8.

Pages 88-90

Mr. Stephenson — Canada — 5 million
Mr. Tanaka — Japan — 4 million
Ms Velasquez — Colombia — 2 million
Mrs. Benelli — Italy — 4 million
Mr. Postma — The Netherlands — 3 million
Miss Olandu — Nigeria — 1 million

Pages 90-91

Tom is the youngest; Reggie is in the middle; Jim is the oldest.

Pages 91-92

Johnson — horseshoe pitching — short, curly hair
Ramsay — weight-lifter — shoulder length, loose hair
Sawchuk — checker player — hair is in a braid
Jacobs — foot racer — short, straight hair, parted in the middle

Pages 95-96

I	E	J	M	A	R	C	H	A	Q
T	X	F	R	I	D	E	G	K	P
O	M	L	G	C	H	A	S	E	D
R	L	O	H	I	K	E	U	D	I
U	V	H	F	B	C	R	E	E	P
O	Y	R	P	A	S	S	Q	M	O
I	P	T	R	O	T	M	J	R	Q
M	Z	P	K	S	W	I	N	G	N
R	S	M	V	B	G	L	I	D	E
W	G	A	L	L	O	P	B	A	L
N	X	U	Q	R	A	C	E	O	F
C	M	C	J	L	Z	O	O	M	N
B	W	N	A	S	P	R	I	N	T
D	T	P	A	C	E	K	D	E	Q
J	N	F	S	T	I	R	K	X	R
G	S	Z	H	B	J	U	M	P	L
H	F	T	G	P	U	S	H	F	P
W	X	D	R	I	V	E	V	P	A
V	V	D	C	C	Y	C	L	E	U
Z	N	L	W	A	L	K	H	K	N
A	I	P	B	S	Q	U	A	K	E
S	X	T	U	R	N	Q	A	P	S
E	U	Q	V	E	X	P	A	N	D
O	T	D	R	I	F	T	C	J	T
V	C	L	I	M	B	P	G	R	U
Y	K	T	R	A	M	P	D	N	I

Pages 98-99

L	F	J	A	H	O	R	N	H	C	I
E	B	A	N	D	R	M	B	G	T	U
O	K	A	J	A	Z	Z	D	L	W	T
U	G	F	T	U	B	A	J	M	O	I
M	X	C	P	I	A	N	O	E	F	X
W	B	B	U	G	L	E	A	O	Z	V
I	T	D	Z	C	H	O	I	R	T	S
X	H	S	I	N	G	K	G	L	Z	Y
S	A	V	L	S	T	R	U	M	D	K
C	O	N	C	E	R	T	B	J	T	W
V	K	H	D	W	H	I	S	T	L	E
L	M	S	A	X	O	P	H	O	N	E
U	J	L	U	L	L	A	B	Y	O	I
O	N	B	A	B	A	S	S	N	Y	C
W	N	L	R	Q	U	A	R	T	E	T
T	N	P	I	P	E	R	D	H	U	K
L	R	H	U	M	B	A	W	Y	E	F
C	S	J	L	Y	R	E	B	G	M	L
V	T	D	U	K	U	L	E	L	E	F
Z	X	X	O	R	G	A	N	V	K	G
Y	A	L	T	O	K	X	E	J	N	U
B	F	C	B	T	E	N	O	R	I	Z
V	K	T	I	Z	I	T	H	E	R	O
L	S	J	G	V	I	O	L	I	N	Z
N	B	A	N	J	O	H	D	C	X	W
Y	E	F	I	F	E	B	N	G	S	M

Pages 100-101

We are in the rapids and must go on.

Pages 102-103

Poker is not a game but an education.

Page 111

Jean is going to the sixth floor.

Page 116

1. 1938 2. 1933 3. 22 4. 10 5. 1928 6. 12

Page 116

Hezekiah was three years old.

Page 117

C
F
D
E
A
B

Page 118

Scotland and Canada

Pages 118-119

Player #35 — 30 points
Player #29 — 21 points
Player #23 — 40 points
Player #3 — 9 points
Player #13 — 10 points
Player #17 — 2 points
Player #7 — 8 points

Player #38 — 48 points
Player #20 — 11 points
Player #8 — 26 points
Player #10 — 8 points
Player #18 — 28 points
Player #6 — 9 points

Team B wins with the score 130 - 120.

Page 120

Y

2	×	5	−	3	= 7
+		−		+	
7	−	4	×	8	= 24
÷		×		×	
3	+	6	×	4	= 36
= 3		= 6		= 44	

3 3 4 4 5 6 7 8

Z

1	+	8	×	2	= 18
×		−		×	
7	×	6	−	9	= 33
+		×		+	
4	−	3	×	7	= 7
= 11		= 6		= 25	

2 3 4 6 7 7 8 9

Page 121

Number the sticks from 1 to 10, from left to right. Make the following five moves: 4 left, 7 left, 5 right, 6 left, 10 left.

Page 121

The sequence in the lines is plus 6, minus 3. Therefore, a is 20 and b is 42.

Page 121

The opposite segments of the wheel are doubled, and then plus or minus one is included alternatively. Therefore, 12 + 12 - 1 = 23; 15 + 15 + 1 = 31; 20 + 20 - 1 = 39 (a); 25 + 25 + 1 = 51 (b).

Page 122

Evelyn wants to play cribbage.

Pages 123-124

1. MNP OML PNL not OLM not NOM not PLO
2. UTR
   If STU and SRU are true — not SUR
   If not STU is true — not UTS SUT
   If STU and TUR are true — RST
   If STU and USR are true — RTU

Page 125

The ox-cart: Simply hypothesize the distance. If the distance is 60 km, then the man could go 30 km by train in 30 minutes and 30 km by ox-cart in 15 hours. If he walked, he would go 60 km in 15 hours. It is faster to walk.

The golf balls: If Peters balances four against four, he will discover the heavier ball among four but will only discover it by luck in his second weigh, by choosing two and balancing them. If one of the two is heavier, then. . . . If not, he has used up his second weigh, and has only narrowed the choice to two. If Peters balances three against three, and the sides balance, then the heavier one is one of the remaining two. Then he needs only to balance them in his second weigh. If the sides do not balance, then the heavier one is one of the balls on the "down" side. He then must balance any two of them. If they are equal, the heavier ball is the one he did not weigh. If one side comes down, then that one is the heavier ball.

Pages 125-126

There are several possible combinations. Here is one:

(a) Sir Harold puts breastplate (25) and shield (10) in basket A and lowers it. Lady B. (40) steps into basket B, goes down, and gets out.

(b) Sir Harold adds helmet (5) to basket A and lowers it. He puts the servant (45) into basket B. The servant goes down and Lady B. rolls him out.

(c) Sir Harold takes the helmet (5) out of basket A and puts in the chain-mail (10). He lowers the basket and Lady B. gets into it. Sir Harold gets into basket B and comes down.

(d) Lady B. takes the shield (10) out of basket A and lowers it. She climbs into basket B and comes down.

Page 127

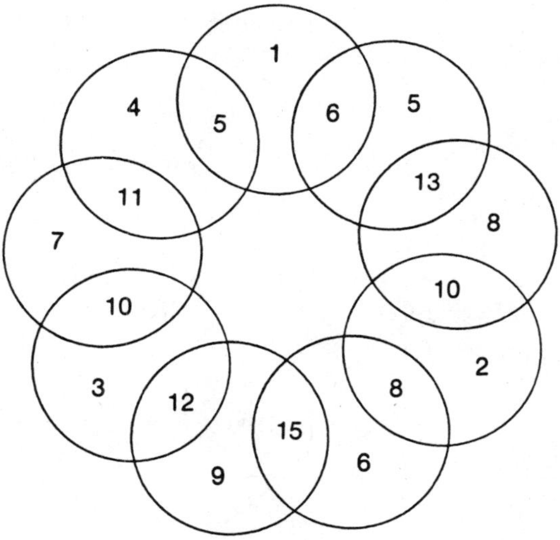

Page 128

Y = 5   Z = 2 or 3 or 6 or 7 or 8   W = 0   V = 1

Page 128

London	Dublin	Copenhagen
Oslo	Rome	Madrid
Lisbon	Berlin	Berne
Paris	Athens	Bonn

Page 134

Dinah — four, Cathy — twelve, Ned — seven, Luis — two

Page 134

grey — 23, red — 22, white — 21, yellow — 24

Page 136

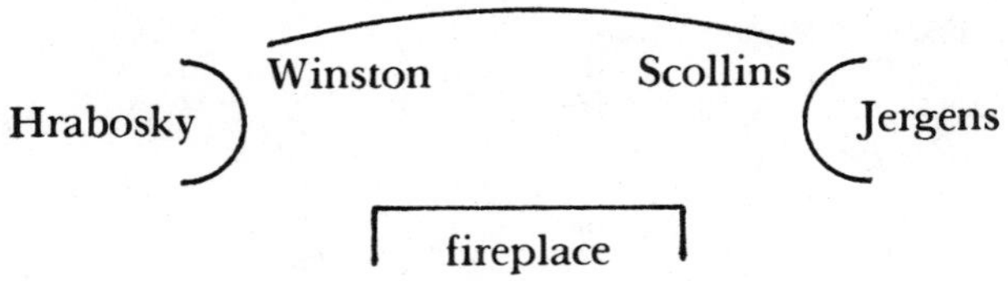

Winston — referee, Hrabosky — magician, Jergens — policeman, Scollins — assassin

Pages 136-137

Stella — (a), Levin — (a) Bonita missed the bus.

Page 141

There are several possibilities. TEAR can be pronounced two ways; HEAR is the only one that is always a verb, etc.

Page 142

TIE is the only one that fits the pattern of consonant-vowel-consonant, consonant-vowel-vowel, etc.

Page 142

ADE is a possibility. If each of the columns is added, and the letters are given value by their position in the alphabet, then the first column adds up to 800, the second to 700, the third to 600. By extension, one would imagine that the fourth column will add up to 500.